SYMBOLS OF
MOROCCO

My heart is scattered throughout the land.
One part is in Marrakech, in a state of uncertainty;
Another in Halfun, another in Meknes, with my books;
Another in the Fazaz, another in Moulouya among my fellow tribesmen,
Another in the Gharb, among my country and city friends
O God, bring them all together, you can, you are the only one who can,
O God, put them all back in their place.

Al-Yousi, *Muhâdarât (The Reason Book)*, 17th century

© 2001 Assouline Publishing
601 West 26th Street, 18th floor
New York, NY 10001
USA
Tel.: 212 989-6810   Fax: 212 647-0005
www.assouline.com

First published by Editions Assouline, Paris, France, 2001

ISBN : 2 84323 293 7

Translated from the French by Simon Pleasance & Fronza Woods.

Color separation: Gravor (Switzerland)
Printed in Italy

Front cover: Marrakech: the Menara. The pleasure pavilion of the Alawite
Sultan Sidi Muhammad (1859-1983), built in 1866, and looking out on its
ornamental pond, measuring 330 x 500 feet. © Philippe Saharoff.
Back cover: The Fantasia: the troop of horsemen. © Philippe Saharoff.

SYMBOLS OF
MOROCCO

XAVIER GIRARD

ASSOULINE

CONTENTS

INTRODUCTION

Morocco forms a huge African peninsula where several geographies and worlds jostle and overlap. In the south, and along the whole of the eastern border, there are vast expanses of desert criss-crossed by *oueds** and oases under serious threat from the advancing Saharan sands. On its western seaboard, the Atlantic coast stretches as far as the eye can see from Cape Spartel in the south to the customs post of Nouadhibou, with its age-old Portuguese and Spanish fortified towns. To the north, seafaring folk come up against the dense and shady Rif ranges, citadel of resistance, soaring above the Mediterranean, from Tetouan to the Spanish enclave Melilla. Then there are the scythe-like slashes created by the Berber mountains, the plateaus of the Middle Atlas, with their harsh, rugged solemnity above Fez; the snow-capped peaks of the High Atlas, visible from Marrakech as they rise sheer out of the Haouz plains; and the arid ridges of the Anti-Atlas, standing tall as though guarding the first approaches to the Sahara.

But Morocco is also a country of lowlands now given over to large-scale farming and thriving *dir*—narrow lands at the foot of the mountains, streaked with vegetable gardens and orchards.

This geographical complexity is matched by the great human diversity of a country with many different languages and dialects, and a host of local traditions. Town- and city-dwelling Moroccans listen to the news in classical Arabic, speak Arabic dialects and French, and, in the south they speak in *hassaniya* Arabic; in the Rif mountains people speak *tarafit*, a berber dialect; in the High and Middle Atlas they speak *tamazight*; and in the High and Anti-Atlas, *tachelhit* (chleuh).

The "tattooed memory" (Abdellatif Khatibi) of Morocco is a mingling of African and Mediterranean legacies and the pre-Islamic heritage and early Islam of the great cities of the East, introduced by Uqba's troops in the 7th century B.C.; the Berber and Arab culture and the refined civilization of the Moors, driven out of Andalusia in 1492; the Sahrawis hailing from the frontiers of sub-Saharan Africa in the 9th century, coming down from the mountains towards Marrakech, and the descendants of Berberized Christians; not forgetting the native Jews, the *toshabim*, present in Morocco from time immemorial, and the *megaroshim*, expelled from Spain between the 14th and the late 15th centuries.

One of the prime symbols of modern Morocco is in Fez, in the confrontation between the mosques of the Kairouan peoples and those of the Andalous, brought together in the 11th century in a "single city" by a sultan (Yusuf ibn Tashufin) born in a tribe hailing from the Sahara, who came from Tripoli in Libya to establish his empire on the shores of the Ebro.

Similarly, it is impossible to talk of a clash between lowland and city-dwelling Arabs, on the one hand, and mountain Berbers, on the other—as the Protectorate was tempted to do at the time of the Berber *dahir* on May 16, 1930. More apposite terms would be Berberized Arabs and Arabized Berbers (or

8

Berberized Jews), who all acknowledged each other as Moroccans. When the Rabti (Rabat's inhabitants) laugh at the inhabitants of Sala or the Casablancans mock the mistakes of the Fassi, one thinks of Neapolitans being derided by Romans, but giving as good as they get.

Nor does the diversity of Morocco mean that the country is enclosed in its series of *riyad* or houses. Old families do still live on, and with them age-old barriers, but this does not mean that they do not communicate with one another. Morocco is not the petrified museum of our exotic imaginations, nor is it the pigeonholed conservatory of a folklore preserved on glossy paper, a picturesque, oriental park and a Third World country rolled into one. No, rather, it is a topographic land of incredible complexity, inviting us to forever switch maps, for old signposts steer visitors straight into pitfalls and misunderstandings.

Yet it's not easy to shed images—and symbols—fashioned by centuries of orientalist literature and painting. The Morocco one visits is a combination of daydreams and "ready-made" pictures.

Many of us are reading books written at the end of the 19th century, as if their brief were to show us the Morocco of the early 21st century. But who can fail to think of Delacroix in front of an open door, and beyond it, where there is an array of *babouches*, or Loti beneath his scented muslin in front of the walls of Fez, or Dumas with his rifle on the beach at Tangier, or Isabele Eberhardt, or the sight of a young woman vanishing beneath her haik in some medina lane, or Saint-Exupéry and his Little Prince, looking at Cap Juby? Who can resist treading in the footsteps of Burroughs, Bowles, Choukri and Genet on the Socco Chico? Who wouldn't make the detour to the Larache cemetery to read the famous tombstone looking out on to the ocean? But aren't we looking for a Morocco that only exists for us?

Sometimes you need chance encounters and the hospitality—far from just mythical—of Moroccans to discover a whole new city, just a few hundred yards from the souk where some guide led you around and not mentioned anywhere, where more than 100,000 marrakchi live, as in Sidi Yusuf Ben Ali, a stone's throw from the Amoravid walls of the "Rose of the South."

Symbols have their history, too. For centuries, the signs of Morocco's recognition were hard to tell apart from some legendary and disconcerting Orient that encompassed Muslim Spain, North Africa and the Ottoman Empire. Those signs that we do retain from reading Pidou de Saint-Olon, Louis XIV's ambassador at the court of Mawlay Ismail, point out the cruel despot and the hugeness of the city's defences, like many a visitor to Baghdad and Damascus in the classical age. For a captive like Germain Mouette and a holy man like father Dan, come to buy back the sultan's slaves, the chastisement meted out to Christians, and the fearsome pirates of Sala are much more vivid symbols than the gardens of the imperial city, which Saint-Olon knew to be of great interest to the Sun King. The picture we make for ourselves of Morocco in the 18th century is that of an "accursed land" filled with wild beasts and fanatics; a mysterious place, closed, hostile and impenetrable. It contrasts sharply with the vision of a "blessed land," of those 16th-century Arab travelers, so fond of fine detail, who, like Leo Africanus, remembered above all, the civilized sumptuousness of the cities and the luxuriant countryside.

When Morocco was no longer threatening, in the 19th century while the Ottoman Empire was crumbling, it faded and darkened. This was the "dark Moghreb" of Loti and Gabriel Charmes, and the "twilight of Islam" of Chevrillon on the eve of the war of conquest. Those were terrible times. Cities were ruined. Their denizens resigned to their fate. Confused decline, vast, perversity of every kind and sudden fits of violence: turn-of-the-century Morocco was—to the eye of the European traveler—"the Sick Man of the West."

Explorers who went there to scout around, from René Caillié to Charles de Foucauld, confirmed this vision of a country at once full of marvels and anarchy, where death lurked. For many, a shroud veiled it like the whitewash of its towns and cities and its blinding skies. The Protectorate hardly changed this repertory of accepted notions about a magnificent but backward Morocco; heir to a very ancient culture, but living in an endless twilight; ruled by a sultan whose person was sacred, but wracked by division, fanaticism and apathy—a country to which France was amply justified in bringing the succor of "civilization."

The symbols that the 20th century will retain are those of a "land of contrasts" illuminated, unlike the Morocco of Pierre Loti, by a dazzling glow of a midday sunset. Photos of the Djebel Toubkal are at their loveliest in spring, when the flowering almond trees glisten with snow. The bright orange-red hue of the walls of Marrakech is not merely photogenic; it fits the image of a flamboyant south highly charged by the shimmering light of the desert and the snow on the Atlas, as in a film. An old man in a *burnous* calls out to a group of children, just as the young woman in her traditional caftan, cell phone clutched to her ear, talks to her girlfriend in Western clothes. Fez and Meknes are inseparable from the art deco of Casa. The tanners of Marrakech, stamping and tramping in those blood-red tanks, are very much from the same country as the luxurious Rabat gallery specializing in design and offering the latest examples of contemporary leatherwork.

The beauty of its imperial cities—a name beckoning dreams of a medieval golden age—the splendors of its *medersas*, its mosques with their minarets embellished with *zelliges*, and its palaces, the untrammelled heritage of its arts and crafts, the treasures of its "riant valleys" and its oases, all bring the rich times of the "Blessed Empire" back to life. Tourism has given Morocco the image of an age-old land with sumptuous landscapes and an old and refined art of living.

But the sweet-scented spirit of *souks* and festivals, the magical atmosphere of Jemaa el-Fna, a meal in the magic spell of a *riyad*, an afternoon spent on the terrace of the Hafa café in Tangier, and the bluish revelations of the Oudaïas casbah in Rabat and the streets of Essaouira, are not the whole picture of Morocco. An attempt to depict what Jacques Berque called "that truth per se of a people and a landscape," being receptive to the sudden events of the moment and those friendly faces, is a sure way of getting closer faster.

When a *sumbolon*, the forebear of the Latin symbol, was handed to the visitor at the entrance to an ancient city, the guest kept one half as a kind of passport, but only the two halves put together after much journeying offered proof that the symbol had been properly used.

* *The Arabian terms are defined in the glossary (p. 138).*

Preceding pages:

Page 4: *High Atlas villages visible from afar in the realm of the Ait Hadidou.*
Their earth-colored roof terraces are created in the same hues as the radiantly
striped landscape. As in the simplest of Berber carpets and rugs, people are
always on the move.

Pages 6-7: *She has intrigued readers of* The Thousand and One Nights,
painters such as Delacroix, Ingres and Matisse, and writers photographing their travels
to the Orient. She is the odalisque, "the woman of the bedchamber"
of bygone Morocco, embellishing harems in the none too distant past.

THE GATE

SPIRIT OF THE THRESHOLD

Morocco is a land of gates. It is separated from Europe by the Gate of Hercules (with Djebel or Mount Tarik of Gibraltar on the European shore and Djebel Moussa on the African shore), and keeps watch over the entrance to the Mediterranean like a "sentinel of Africa." For the Arabs, the Strait of Gibraltar is the Bab al-Zaka, the Narrow Gate, on the route of empire. For European visitors, it is the westernmost gate of Islam, whose eastern counterpart is the Sublime Gate, the Ottoman Empire.

On its western flank, tourist guides take you as far as the "gateway to the desert." Taza is the gate people must pass through on their way from eastern to western Morocco. Marrakech is the "gateway to the south," also known as the "gateway to Africa." For many centuries, Morocco has been compared to a fortress hidden by its mountains, deserts and rugged shores, communicating with the world solely through rare breaches, carefully guarded and manned.

When the 19th-century traveler reached Tangier, he was still not altogether in Morocco. For Pierre Loti, the real gateway to the ancient Empire lay much further inland, at Fez, "deep in that motionless land, closed to life."[1] To get there, he had to pass through a series of gates, undergo the repeated rite of entrance on the divided soil of dissident tribes—the Beni-Malek, the Beni-Hassem, the Zemmour, the Cherarbas and the Zerhouas—negotiate natural obstacles like the Oued Sebou, that "boundary hewn between this Morocco and that Morocco,"[2] plunge into time and space, and crawl back toward the "human cat-flap" of his austere house in Fez.

In the first town he came upon, Ksar-al-Kebir, he ventured "through a series of old ogival gates"[3] shaped in the Portuguese ramparts by the Arabs. Then he would leave the town through other "arches, misshapen and lopsided, but always with delightful shapes and delicate frames."[4] In Fez, a gate made up of several arches leads to "another gate, just as huge but all white and fresh, ringed by blue and pink mosaics and arabesques," like the "gate to some enchanted palace."[5] Elsewhere, "a triple ogival gate, contorted, thick and deep, in every way like the one at the Alhambra,"[6] bedazzled him. The gates and doors to his ancient home in Fez were probably low, narrow and very old, but he was most fond of them, as if they finally offered him a brief glimpse of that "dark Moghreb" he had come to discover.

But, like most travelers, Loti said little about the role of city gates. Arab chroniclers, on the other hand, viewed them with a keen eye: of Morocco (Marrakech), Leo Africanus said, "It had 24 gates and very beautiful and very strong walls, built of chalk adobe and coarse sand mixed with gravel."[7] The number of gates here is important, for this is what pointed to the greatness of the city and gave a good idea of its magnificence. It is by the number and scale of its gates, too, that Meknes measures itself against other Islamic cities. Above the Bab al-Mansour, you can read a cuneiform inscription to the glory of Mawlay

12

With its horseshoe arch, overlaid frames, carved spandrels, decoratively inscribed lintel, decor of pilasters and enameled tiles, the gate is the prime symbol of the city and an emblem of its fortune.

Ismail and his son "through whom Islam appeared holding firm the standard of the crown," and specifically mentioning "that no monument in Damascus is as ornate as Alexandria, which has the glory of unforgettable columns and porticos, unmatched for their beauty." Gates with horseshoe arches, bequeathed by the Roman Empire, inscribed and decorated with floral and geometric motifs and lined with *zelliges* and carved stones, add to the city's prestige: "In all Meknes," noted Henri Bosco about Bab al-Mansour, "that is all you see. It is there when you arrive. It is the colossal gate. When you have left, it is it that you remember, and nothing else."[8]

Unlike the anonymous gates and doors of houses, city gates must be clearly identified. They proclaim themselves loud and clear, like Bab al-Khemis in Fez, which declares in Kufic script above its arch: "I am the lucky gate, akin, in my splendor, to the full moon. I was built by Mawlay Ismail. Good luck and prosperity are inscribed upon my brow. I am surrounded by happiness."

Through its gates, the city must demand respect, provoke admiration and fear, and make its personality and its ambition as clear as day. The name of each particular gate is known to all. Some gates of imperial cities have been named after the day on which the nearby market is held (there are plenty called Bab al-Khemis, the Thursday gates, and Bab al-Had, the Sunday gates): Others are associated with a specialty market like Bab al-Berdain in Fez (the pack-saddle gate) or an activity like Bab al-Debbagh (the tanners' gate); others still are given a personal touch by the air that swirls around them, as in the numerous Bab al-Rouahs, wind gates, that you find in Fez, Meknes and Rabat. Some gates are named for a place of worship, a devotion, a patronage or a glorious memory, while many are linked with a right of passage or a specific use, like Bab al-Robb in Fez (the grape gate or the heated-wine gate), close to the mellah—the only gate permitting wine to enter the city—or Bab al-Makhzen, in Marrakech, once the sultan's gate. One of the most sumptuous and famous gates in all Morocco, Bab Agnaou, in Marrakech, right beside another Bab al-Robb, is named for a Berber legend: the gate of the ram with neither horn nor voice.

A few stand in memory of the fees that had to be paid when one entered the city, or to the forbears of the "hygiene inspections" that were carried out beneath their vaults. Every evening, until the early part of the 20th century, the city would shut itself in behind its stout and studded portals, bolting the inner gates leading to each of its neighborhoods and districts.

The inner door. Inside the home, the cedar door is also a feature of special veneration. Whether carved or painted, it is a protective boundary, a family luxury, the partition that is pulled shut on the room which was open all day long, and the guardian of the horma.

THE IMPERIAL CITY

THE SULTAN'S CITY

Fez, Marrakech, Meknes and Rabat are all "imperial cities." The term originally refered to the area occupied by the Dar al-Makhzen, the royal palaces and their compounds accommodating the sultan and the entourage of officials to the royal household, the *mokhazni*. Guides in Meknes use the term "imperial city" to describe the closed and partitioned perimeter where Mawlay Ismail (1672–1727) had his palaces built, along with an *aguedal*, a *mechouar*, mosques and *medersa*, stables and huge storehouses.

The word harks back to the period between the 8th and 13th centuries, when Morocco's sovereignty extended from the shores of the Atlantic to the Gulf of Sirte, and from the southern reaches of the western Sahara to the Ebro valley in Al-Andalus land (now Andalusia).

The first city was Fez, founded in the early 9th century by Idriss Ibn Abdallah and his son Mawlay Idriss, modeled on the main centers of the Islamic civilization: Baghdad in the reign of the Abbassid dynasty and Damascus under the Umayyad dynasty.

The second, Marrakech, built of dried mud like a *ksar* of the Tafilalet, was a Saharan creation, the brainchild of Yusuf ibn Tashufin, the first Almoravid sultan, hailing from the outskirts of the desert and arriving via the valleys of the Atlas ranges in the middle of the 11th century. There, according to Leo Africanus, he established "the presidial seat of all his realm."

Meknes is an "archipelago city" built amidst olives and fruit trees. It dates back to the pre-Islamic period, the *jahilya*. Mawlay Ismail, brother of the founder of the Alawite dynasty, Mawlay Rachid, turned it into his fortress-capital in the 17th century.

Rabat was a Carthaginian trading post that became a Roman colony known as Sala Colonia. It stood on the site of present-day Shella, on the frontiers of the Empire, and the junction of three entities: the city of Sala, the Rabat headland and the Andalusian city.

But if all these were *makhzeniyia* cities, they were not all centers of civilization boasting a high degree of refinement and their own particular urban culture. Marrakech and Meknes are no match for Fez. Their rural and nomadic origins mark them as *badiya* cities, somewhat coarse. Their "drifting population" was too large and their bonds with the countryside too strong for them to be on the same level as the "supreme cities," Baghdad and Damascus. They were not *hadariyya* cities, with an ancient city culture, a religious élite, an established university and a solid middle class. Tetouan, which is not an imperial city and which consistently withstood the power of the *Makhzen*, was hadariyya because the Andalous, who took refuge there in the early years of the 16th century, re-created the refinement of the cities of Muslim Spain. Rabat-Sala would not become hadariyya until the 19th century, when the wealth and the aristocratic distinction of the city clouded its Barbary origins.

Fez. Most unusual, the Athens of Africa, the country's first imperial city: the names given to Fez, rivaling Cordoba, Damascus and Baghdad, clearly convey the splendors of the Merinid capital, and the prestige it still enjoys.

Fez proudly calls itself the prototype of the Islamic city. "This is how Cordoba must have been, in the days of the Caliphate," wrote Gomez Carillo, "and Seville in the time of Almanzor, and Granada, too, at its height."[1]

Le Fassi, who often saw himself as an example of the typical city-dweller, described Fez as the "sole city" of Morocco. The foundation of Fez in 808 made it the first capital. In those early days after its founding, it ruled over a fragile "kingdom of Fez," at war on all sides with the Bled es-Siba, the unsubdued land.

The city, like Meknes and Rabat-Sala, came into being through the linking of distinct groups: Berbers, Kairouanese and Andalous, all of whom wasted no time in declaring war. Two casbahs, two mosques (the Qaraouine and the Andalouse), two medinas, and two cultures were pitted against each other, and developed a reciprocal hatred until the 11th century, when Yusuf ibn Tashufin, founder of the Almoravid dynasty who made Marrakech his capital, managed to unite the two cities and construct a military base there. In the 12th century, the Almohads encircled it with walls and ramparts and succeeded in joining the two sides. But it was under the Merinid sultans, Abu Hassan and his son Abu Inan, in the following century, that Fez, by then once more capital of the kingdom, enjoyed a boom. In 1276, in the reign of Abu Yusuf Yaqub (1258-1286), the city incorporated a new city, Fez al-Jedid. The ancient, middle-class and mercantile medina, Fez al-Bali, was flanked by an administrative and military city, and a large Jewish quarter. Fez enjoyed its golden age. it was the great trading city of western Islam and the real intellectual and religious hub of Morocco.

As a northern city born under the combined sign of the Orient and Muslim Spain, Fez was—as Raffaele Cattedra observed, a "city of membership."[2] Marrakech was quite different: the southern capital, "the great fondouq of Morocco," was open to every manner of trade, and didn't belong entirely to any of the worlds that met there: the Berber mountains, the Sahara desert or the lowland civilization. Hailing from Sous, with the tribes of northern Mauritania, Yusuf ibn Tashufin set up his camp there in 1057, after stopping at Aghmat on the Ourika river. He pitched his tent on this spot, built a mosque and a casbah, and brought in water with the help of a system of kettara—underground pipes. In 1082, he became lord of the western Maghreb, as far as Kabylia, and embarked on the reconquest of Muslim Spain. In 1126, Ali ibn Yusuf, his son, constructed a ten-mile wall in eight months to protect the city from raiding Masmouda Berbers. The old military encampment became an imperial capital. In the early 12th century, in the footsteps of a Masmouda mahdi named Ibn Tumart, who preached for reform against the Almoravids, Abd al-Mumin, a Berber belonging to the Zenata tribe, drove the Almoravids out of Marrakech and founded the Almohad dynasty, which reigned for a hundred years over an empire stretching from Castile to Tripoli.

Built on the ancient Almoravid palace, the mosque and minaret of the Koutoubia served as prototypes for the Giralda in Seville and the Hassane Tower in Rabat. In 1269, the Merinids caused Marrakech to lose its status of capital, which the city had enjoyed for two centuries, in favor of Fez. The Saadians, from the Draa valley, put an end to their reign in the mid-16th century, and reinstated Marrakech in its role as capital. In 1578, Al-Mansur al-Dehebi started work on the construction of the Al-Bedi palace, a huge four-sided edifice clad in marble and onyx. But this renaissance was challenged in the 17th century by Mawlay Ismail, who loathed Marrakech at least as much as Fez, and carved up the Bedi palace.

Marrakech regained the prestigious image of the Almoravids and the Almohads in the 19th century, when the sultans in power had the Bahia palace built, and the great gardens restored. The Menara pavilion dates from that period when "the old mythical city," as Balthasar Porcel[3] calls it, tried to recreate its golden heyday. In the mid-20th century, the city where Doris Day and James Stewart found adventure in Alfred Hitchcock's *The Man Who Knew Too Much* was little more, in the Western view, than a dangerous city bristling with shady people. Since then, the image of a luxurious city has swept away the old cliches. "While Fez remains secret and dark," writes Brice Matthieussent, "Marrakech is a city of light and open air. You can see Fez as thrilling, but also alien and at times hostile. In Marrakech, you let the movement and joy sweep you along. The whole city has taken on the character of its people; the straightforward and gentle warmth and friendliness of people of the south."[4]

Mawlay Ismail turned Meknes into a stronghold with walls of dizzying height. He alone represents the entire history of the city. Yet behind the colossal defensive provisions, the age-old archipelago of lesser cities survived and spread. Meknes-of-the-olives, Miknasset al-Zitoun, has not turned its back on its nomadic, tree-growing origins. The city recalls the time when the Miknassa, a Berber tribe coming from the Moulouya, set up home on the banks of the Oued Bou Fekran, to grow vines and fruit trees. Leo Africanus saw it as "lovely, abundant, well enclosed and very strong, with beautiful streets, well aired and agreeable."[5]

When Mawlay Ismail succeeded Mawlay Rachid in 1673, in the early days of the Alawite monarchy, the city was no longer the orchard described by Leo Africanus. Upheavals had wreaked havoc in the empire at the end of Al Andalus in the 15th century, and the gradual decline in the 16th century did not spare Meknes. It became an imperial capital ruling over territories that extended from the Atlantic and Mediterranean ports to the plains of Sudan.

Like Meknes and Fez, Rabat-Sala is an archipelago city. Originally Carthaginian, then Roman, ancient pre-Islamic Shella is just a romantic cemetery today, with its Abul Hassan mosque, its holy pool and its

koubba in ruins. Sala, the port city built on the right bank of the Bou Regreg from the 11th century on, was a vast *medina* encircled by ochre walls, that used to open on to kitchen gardens, with Bab al-Mrisa— the gate of the little harbor—designed to let boats and vessels through. Its name is associated with the piracy that thrived here from the early years of the 17th century until 1829, on the eve of the capture of Algiers by French troops. The pirates set up their lair in "new Sala"—present-day Rabat—built on the other bank. Rabat is named after the rock of the Oudaias, where, in the 12th century Almohad period, Abd al-Mumin built a fortified monastery, which would be turned into a military camp before long, and where, not far away, in 1197, Yakub al-Mansur had ordered the construction of a mosque which was to be larger than all the other mosques in Islam—except Samara. The city had no more than a hundred or so houses when Leo Africanus passed through it, which left our traveler "wonderfully moved to pity." Its rebirth in the 17th century was due to Moors—the Hornacheros—who, in fleeing from Extremadura, found refuge in 1608 in the old casbah. A few years later, a second wave of expulsions and the arrival of the La Marmora pirates gave birth to the city of the Andalous, which would be called Sala the New, built on land at the foot of the fortified city. Today, as Lyautey noted, Rabat is "the Washington, D.C. of Morocco, with Casablanca its New York." The capital city, seat of the king, ministries and embassies, as well as many universities, is one of the hubs of artistic and intellectual life of Morocco.

Preceding pages: *Marrakech: the walls. Erected in 18 months, in 1126 and 1127,*
under the reign of Ali ibn Yusuf, last of the Almoravid sultans, to protect Marrakech from Almohad forays
and continually altered ever since, the walls of the red city have foiled every attempt to destroy them.
Opposite: *Rabat. The casbah of the Oudaïs seen from the Bou Regreg: Nowadays,*
the ancient city of the Hornacheros pirates is a hive of tourism, where visitors cannot avoid the Rue Jemaa,
the pirates' tower, the Moorish café and the Andalusian-style garden of the Museum of Moroccan Arts.

TANGIER

LAND OF PASSAGE

The Greeks called it Tingis; Leo Africanus, Tangia; the Portuguese, Tangiarra. In the Berber tongue, Tangier is Tinji, and in Arabic, Tan'ja, or "land retrieved." "Land! Land!," "Tindji! Tindji!," the people in Noah's Ark exclaimed when they saw Cape Malabata .[1]

Tanga, wife or daughter of Antaeus, comes from the legend of Hercules. A Roman ceramic in the *casbah* museum spells it out loud and clear: "Here is Tanga, once founded by Antaeus." After this feat, and a sojourn in the garden of the Hesperidies, where he made off with fruit of the bitter orange tree, Hercules rested in the grottoes of Cape Spartel, where rickety "Tungis Buses" now take you from the Grand Socco. Tangier's first visitors where Phoenicians. Then came the Carthaginians. The Romans turned it into a stronghold at the confluence of the "two seas" and one of the capitals—along with Caesaria—of Tingitan Mauretania. You would take the road to Volubilis and Sala Colonia (Rabat). Precious little remains of that Roman Tingis, which was ravaged by the Vandals in 429, and just about as little of the Byzantine and Visigoth city, too.

In 707, the city put up schools and mosques. In 711, it took part in the conquest of Spain alongside Ceuta, and became one of the Ben al-Medjaz, a "port of the land of passage" of the Empire. From then on, in its ideal position, it was the check point of Muslim Spain and the "Kingdom of Morocco," and lived through the highs and lows of the Al-Andalus adventure. From 1471 to 1578, the Portuguese made it their home until they were ousted by the Spanish after the Battle of the three Kings. The English then occupied it, before being driven out in 1684 by Mawlay Ismail, who, while he was at it, also retook Larache and Asilah.

The city's awakening dates back to the end of the 18th century, when the sultan brought together various consulates scattered between Mogador and Rabat. Until the beginning of the 20th century, the city was the diplomatic gateway to Morocco, the threshold where the foreigner was admitted but kept at arm's length. For the Moroccan from the interior, it would henceforth be the "city of dogs," *madinat al-kelba*; a place which the presence of "wetbacks"—Europeans—laid bare every manner of depravity and traffic. The consuls were well aware of this, and reluctantly set up home in Tangier.

In the 19th century, there were about a dozen of them, staving off their boredom on the fringes of the Petit Socco and Rue Siaghine, where the sultan's representative, the *Naïb*, had his residence. Before long, the diplomatic city attracted a mini-society with some oddball stars: a *Times* journalist named Walter Harris, an English nanny, wife of the sheriff of Ouezanne, one Miss Emily Keene, and, some decades later, David Herbert, an eccentric lord. There was Barbara Hutton too, and a host of semi-retired celebrities. Classified as an "international zone" with "special status" as a free city placed under the authority of a council of rep-

The city seen from the heights of the casbah; in the distance, the oued Moghagha, cape Malabata, and the foothills of the Rif mountains.
White Tangier, Tangier of black money, Tangier where smugglers of illegal aliens thrive—"dream city" and town of Choukri's "Naked Bread."

resentatives from nine countries, from 1924 to 1940 Tangier was the exchange and espionage capital of North Africa, the radiant city for all kinds of wheeling and dealing.

As the years passed, the number of foreigners swelled. At the end of the 19th century there were 3,500 foreigners, residents of this "mini-Europe." Seasonal visitors also increased. But above all writers came, arriving by steamship from Algeciras and Marseilles, like Edmondo de Amicis in 1876, or Pierre Loti in 1889. Journalists, like Mark Twain came in 1867 and Gabriel Chares in 1887; and pilgrims keen to add an opus to their oeuvre, like Alexandre Dumas in 1846, and recently Paul Theroux.

After Delacroix's visit in 1832, the list of painters who followed one another to Tangier grew ever larger: Dehodencq in 1853, Henri Regnault and Clairin in 1869, Benjamin Constant in 1870, and countless numbers of orientalists from every part of Europe. When Matisse stayed in Tangier in 1912 and 1913, he was obeying an already ancient tradition that carried on after him. "Because of them," wrote Jean Louis Miège, "Tangier was seen before being known, then known as they had shown it. Nowhere did reality end up looking so much like the art it had inspired."[2] From the moment of arrival, the visitor of Tangier, heads not so much into a tourist city as into the pages of some exotic novel. In the 1950s, William Burroughs, drawn by that "terminus of dope" to which he had been summoned by Brian Gysin, hung out in the Muniriya Hotel, writing *Naked Lunch* and *Interzone*. Allen Ginsberg and Gregory Corso crossed paths in Tangier with Truman Capote, Gore Vidal, Alec Waugh, Gavin Young, John Hopkins and Tennessee Williams. The 1960s played host to Jean Genet, Samuel Beckett and Roland Barthes.

But the "mirage capital" would not have touched our imaginations if Paul Bowles hadn't landed there in 1931, with the composer Aaron Copland; and if he hadn't decided to set up home there with Jane Auer from 1947 on; and if Moroccan writers such as Mohamed Choukri and Mohamed Mrabet hadn't also gathered around him.

As a metropolis with almost a million inhabitants, where illegal immigrants rub shoulders with lovers of all that isn't quite "above board,"[3] Tangier is nostalgic for the dream city of yesterday. But, as Robert Briatte writes, "Tangier is an essentially anachronistic city, it is always a survival of something, precisely when that something no longer exists, or one no longer manages to put a name to it."[4]

Youth. Half of Morocco's population—now almost 35,000,000 strong—is under 15. Urban children and teenagers are the symbol of the country, an explosive symbol where youthful energy and exuberance by no means necessarily lead to the possibility of a job and somewhere to live.

JEMAA EL-FNA

THE WORLD'S SQUARE

From the terrace of the Café de France hotel, travelers will discover the Jemaa el-Fna square. Guidebooks strongly recommend stationing oneself there at sundown to take in the whole scene: the *medina*, the minaret of the Koutoubia and, in the distance, the oasis in the direction of the Gueliz mountains.

The Spanish writer Juan Goytisolo consulted other guides, like Fodor's, which recommend discovering the square in the morning, or getting to know it unexpectedly, but, as our Marrakech-lover observes, "all the guides have got it wrong—there's no way you can catch it."[1]

At our traveler's feet, the "square where there is every kind of traffic," the "square of sharing," the "crazy square" is filled with a silent throng. Rings of people around storytellers, magicians, snake-charmers, tumblers and jugglers, mimes and acrobats, dancers and musicians have formed in the flickering glow of hurricane lamps. Gusts smelling of grilled meat rise up to the café terrace. For a few *dirhams*, an expanse of people in the square are getting ready to gobble up kebabs and spicy salads, *harira*, mountains of giblets, and sheep heads, all washed down with glasses of green tea. The traveler lends an ear to the hubbub of this huge night market, this incredible sizzling vibration, to try and make out in all the music and honking horns, the shrill sound of the *qraqech*, a type of metallic rattle, the *bendir* and his bagpipe-like lament, the tom-tom of big *gangas*, the large African drum and the droning trill of the *guenbri*, banjos with three strings of goat gut, played by the *Gnaoua* minstrel.

Near the medina, orange and date vendors beneath their striped awnings light the square's outer rim. But the crowd stays plunged in obscurity, as if people came here to stock up on darkness.

On summer evenings, on Jemaa el-Fna, the "boys of the shadows," as they are called by their Machreq neighbors, devour the night with the same gusto as the Andalous. In the setting sun, the half-Spanish, half-Moorish silhouette of the Koutoubia surveys the scene from its gilded globes.

Tourists, students, soldiers on leave, country folk from the Haouz, mountain dwellers from the Atlas and street kids have all come to witness a spectacle that resembles an octopus. In a splendid and succinct meditation on life on Jemaa el-Fna, José Angel Valente notes that, in front of this throng that you don't hear, the visitor is "poised at the beginning of a dream, without venturing into it," a dream in which "everything can suddenly be erased,"[2] like Giorgio de Chirico's deserted city squares.

"North Africa's leading tourist attraction," as Arthur Koestler put it, the Jemaa el-Fna, center of Morocco's legends and roadside cuisine, recently listed as a world oral culture site, is the country's largest popular meeting place.

THE SOUK

MARKET PLACES

It's *lioum souk*, market day. From four in the morning, the roads leading to Morocco's country markets have been busy. There's no time to waste. Buses, trucks and vans, all overloaded and belching fumes, donkeys beneath the *chouari*, the bulging sack, scooters and taxis, trunks crudely tied down with string, they must all get there on time. The *souk* may sometimes be 40 miles from the *douar*, where market-goers must return the same evening. Week after week, it's the same *harka*. A 1975 survey listed 850, and reckoned their nomadic population to be three million.[1] They are no less numerous today, flocking to the canvas village pitched in the middle of the desert or on the outskirts of towns, not counting the permanent markets in large cities. The first deals have to do with livestock. Then it's poultry; rush hour for vegetables is later; sometimes it's all over by early afternoon, but permanent markets never close before nightfall. Despite the recent appearance of "supermarkets," one thing is clear: "The souk is an institution that's very much alive and kicking," observes Jean-François Troin, "and one we must be sure not to reduce to the rank of some historical memory. It's like a unique magnet for people of the *bled*, a special forum for city merchants' businesses, a festival that comes round week in week out, like an essential cog in Morocco's rural life."[2]

The largest souks call to mind the vast markets of Africa, which are perhaps the closest models. In the middle, cloth merchants set up their stalls by tea stands and spice traders, as in the covered district of the *qissariya*—clothing markets—of Fez and Meknes, which are closed at night. Nearby, hosiers, men's clothing and *babouche* vendors set up shop. The second area, for fruit and vegetables, is side by side with the cafés, "tea tents" and kebob vendors. In country markets, butchers' stalls are right next to the still-fuming slaughterhouse. Close by, the alleys are filled with poultry which tourists in the Meknes souk find hard to swallow, so to speak. On the outer edges, the maze becomes less dense, peasants spread out their wares on mats and barbers ply their trade. The most famous souks, those of Fez and Marrakech, fan out, depending on particular crafts and trades: the blacksmiths' souk, souks of stone-dressers, leather-workers and basket-makers. You can never leave the great souks of Morocco without wanting to get lost in them once more, with no aim other than wandering through their overlapping byways, as if in a kaleidoscope.

Opposite: *The city souk. The magic of the souk is a rush of spicy aromas, raucous cries, light-filtering palms and colorful fabrics, glancing eyes and exclamations, as well as a billion things manufactured within arm's reach and a maze of lanes where getting lost is fun.*
Following pages: *The country souk. Weekly souks are first and foremost like tent towns set up in the outskirts of cities or in open country—a world that is more organized than might appear at first glance. These souks are veritable economic hubs in the lives of Morocco's present-day countryfolk.*

THE MELLAH

THE JEWS OF MOROCCO

The presence of Jews in Maghreb from the 6th century B.C. on has given rise to all kinds of legends. A Roman inscription at Volubilis is the first confirmed sign of their settlement in Morocco. One thing is certain: the *toshabim*, or native Jews, were in Shella and Al Jedida and throughout northern Morocco when Uqbah's troops arrived in A.D. 683.

Islam, which had given the Jews cause to fear for their safety, turned out to be more tolerant than the Visigoths of Spain and the Maghreb, and definitely more liberal towards the Ashkenazi than the Christian West. In 634, a decree issued by the Caliph Omar declared them—just like Christians—*dhimmi* or protected: "Their rights are ours, their obligations are ours"; in principle, Jewish possessions and persons would be respected.[1]

Despite rashes of victimization (having to wear dark clothing, remove their shoes by mosques and holy places, not being allowed to bear arms, or travel on horse or donkey in towns and cities, etc.), sporadic outbreaks of persecution (on the death of the sultan) and one or two generally grim periods—under the Almohads, for example, who did away with the Dhimma, drove them out of major cities, or forced them to convert to Islam—the Jews would, for centuries, be an integral part of economic and cultural life in Morocco. Moroccos' toshabim population is essentially city-dwelling, made up of shopkeepers, craftsmen, peddlars plying their trades in *qissariya* and *souks*. Many professions—doctors, lawyers and teachers (like Maimonides),[2] apothecaries, bankers and businessmen—are traditionally practiced by Jews. "There are Jews in all the good cities of the States of the King of Morocco," observed Germain Moüette at the end of the 17th century, "and it is they who conduct all the business."[3]

The Jews on "the other shore" were in contact with the eastern Mediterranean, and thereby formed the bridgehead for trade with Muslim Spain. Fully-fledged partnerships sprang up, based on the links they managed to keep with their old homeland between Fez and Cordoba, Ceuta and Lucena, Tetouan and Granada. From the late 14th century on, many Jews from Seville found refuge in Morocco. At the beginning of the 15th century, they were sufficiently numerous to be driven out of the *medina* in Fez and forced to settle in the city neighborhood that contained salt warehouses (*mehl*), which was duly known as the mellah. From then on, the term would be used to describe all Jewish quarters in Morocco.

In 1421, the first *mellah* in Morocco, built away from the Arab city (but before long incorporated within its walls), was constructed in Fez, with its very own walls and gates, which were closed every night. In no time, it proved to be too small to accommodate the successive waves of *megourashim*, the Jews who had been expelled from Spain, driven out by Isabella the Catholic and Ferdinand between 1492 and 1497. This influx of some 300,000 Castilian-speaking Jews, heirs to a refined culture and well versed in

A street in the mellah. The mellah or Jewish quarter is just a memory these days. It used to be inhabited by a community that was one of the most important in North Africa—a community associated with all the country's historical events, from the 15th century to the creation of the state of Israel, and the wholesale exodus of 1967.

doing business with the Levant, included great lawyers, geographers, mathematicians, poets and artists. This produced nothing less than an intellectual and commercial renaissance which was advantageous to Morocco's other imperial cities. These cities duly built their mellah over the ensuing centuries—1557 in Marrakech, 1679 in Meknes, 1765 in Essaouira, and 1808 in Rabat-Sala. Before long, new mellah were added to the original quarters to house a population which, in the wake of the Second World War, was as large as in the heyday after their expulsion from Spain.

If you stroll down Rue Bou Khessiat or the imposing Rue des Mérinides that ran through the mellah of Fez, or along the neglected lanes of the Marrakech mellah between the Derb al Badi and the Bahia palace, or through the old and new mellah of Meknes (the latter built in 1930) near Bab Khemis—now lived in by Arab families—it is difficult to get a sense of the busy, thriving life that went on in the Jewish quarter before the end of the mellah, in 1967. All that remains is the rectilinear alignment of the streets, the facades with their windows, the corbels, the wooden balconies and Andalusian bars. Ancient synagogues are now turned into sports centers and mosques.

Pidou de Saint-Olon noted in Meknes, shortly after the construction of the mellah: "It is quite a large neighborhood, no more salubrious than in other cities. The Jews are always at ease indoors, and invariably enjoy more comfort than the Moors themselves."[4] Two centuries later, European travellers would describe it quite differently, smugly emphasizing the "Jewish inferno." Loti stopped off at the gate to the mellah in Fez, repelled by "the general dumping of dead animals (a courtesy accorded them)"[5] creating a stench on the outskirts. For the Tharaud brothers, who visited it in the 1910s, the mellah of Fez was a "venomous" spot, "one of the most awful spots in the world" and "filthier than ever"[6], hence the dream of its occupants of going to live in the Europeans' city, a "1930 mellah."

A quite different verdict was pronounced by Edmond Amran El Maleh on the mellah of Essaouira: "If you cling to the traditional image of the mellah, product of sickly thinking, infested with ideology, a murky place reeking of humiliation, squalid poverty and degradation, then nothing of the sort exists, either at Essaouira-Mogador or at Safi, and not in any respect."[7] But these days all that remains of that world of Moroccan mellah is the living memory of writers and poets. The last Jews in Morocco, who number about 8,000, live for the most part in Casablanca.

Young Jewish woman. A society nurtured on Andalusian and eastern culture and open to the Mediterranean world;
proud of its riches and its art of living. Today, literature, music, fine food and traditional arts and crafts have all survived the end of the mellahs.

THE MOSQUE

PLACE OF GATHERING AND PRAYER

Compared to the great mosques of the Ottoman Empire and Iran, the mosques of Morocco have often been looked at with a dash of disdain. Apart from the Qaraouine of Fez, none of them can compete, in terms of seniority, architectural splendor and teaching reputation with the great mosques of Damascus (706-715), Cordoba (785), Cairo (859) or, in the Maghreb, with the mosque of Kairouan, in Tunisia (836). When European art historians and archaeologists responded to Lyautey's plea and in the early days of the French Protectorate embarked on an inventory of the artistic heritage of the realm, their principal interest actually lay elsewhere. As Henri Terrasse writes: "At that time we were spellbound by the discovery of the *medersas*; alongside these fragile and luxurious wonders with their harmonious perfection, mosques which could only boast ruined walls, white naves with cumbersome pillars, glimpsed through a half-open door or gate, and minarets almost all with no decoration, could only be buildings of secondary importance, invariably doomed to poverty [....]. People forgot," Henri Terrasse adds, "that it is unwise to pass judgement on buildings which you do not venture into."[1]

When Pierre Loti was taken to the vicinity of the Qaraouine (857), he asked his guide: "That's it, isn't it? That's Qaraouine, the holy mosque, the Mecca of all the Maghreb where, for ten centuries or so, they've preached war on the infidel [..]. For centuries they've been accumulating riches of every sort, and thoroughly mysterious things come to pass within. Through the arched gate, we can glimpse vague distant columns and arcades, with exquisite and delightful shapes, festooned with the wonderful art of the Arabs."[2]

The mosque, merely glimpsed, lit by "a million lamps spreading a snowy whiteness" is a fabulous place. For the Tharaud brothers it had lost none of its splendor "with its bronze doors, its black and white paved floor, the stream trickling through it, the fountain for ablutions, so perfectly elegant, its nave with three hundred pillars and countless lamps,"[3] but in the 1910s it was no longer the intellectual hub that drew Gerbert d'Aurillac, Ibn al-Arabi, Ibn Batuta and Ibn Khaldun. The Qaraouine they describe has become a "tomb of the spirit," evidence of the decay into which Morocco had fallen at the dawn of the 20th century. Off-limits to non-Muslims, it can only be the symbol of an exclusive religion, the "hub of fanaticism" of the most barbaric variety. These days, all that unsuspecting tourists see of it is a door giving onto a bed of carpets and mats beneath a forest of columns.

For the religiously-inclined Moroccan, the mosque is a familiar place sometimes quite close to where he works. He will go to it several times a day, long enough for a ritual prayer, a discussion or a siesta. For such purposes there is no need for him to go to the main mosque, which is where he heads on Fridays for the great prayer service. Every other day of the week the local *masjid* will do, or, even more modestly, a

Casablanca: Hassan II mosque. The Hassan II mosque, designed by French architect Michel Pinseau and built by the Bouygues company, is the grandiose manifesto of the neotraditional aesthetic that inspired the monarch's architectural policy from the 1970s onward.

simple room, a *msid*, with no minaret. This latter is often located in the *souk*, its entrance barely distin-
guishable from the shop next door or the *hammam*, whose green door may at times be more conspicuous
with its ceramic surrounds and the plaque bearing its name, opening hours and foundation date. You can
spot the entrance to the msid, by the slight bustle, and the lines of shoes not far from the threshold.
Moroccan mosques that open their doors to visitors are a bit different: you enter them to visit a monument, such as the mausoleum of Mawlay Ismail in Fez, with its series of lofty ochre rooms open to the
sky, leading across a *zellige* carpet to the sovereign's tomb, or the Arab-Andalusian mosque of Tinmal built
in the early 12th century by Abd al-Mumin in the High Atlas valley, a somewhat forbidding four-sided
edifice of pale stone that calls to mind the early days of the Almohad reform. When it comes to the
Qaraouine or the mosque of the Andalous (859) in Fez, the visitor hardly sees more than Pierre Loti did,
and has to imagine the oblong courtyard covered with zelliges, its two Saadian kiosks copied from the
Lion Court at the Alhambra, and the half-Spanish, half-Moorish sumptuousness of the *minbar*—the oldest in Morocco—along with the 18 portals and the library created in the 14th century, which contains
some of the rarest manuscripts in the Arab world. At the Koutoubia in Marrakech he will not be able to
visit the huge trapezoid hall, its seven spans and its domes, but will have to be content with the minaret,
its turquoise friezes, its delicate Andalusian arcatures and its pink rag-stones from Gueliz, back-lit by a
sun setting on the four golden globes of its famous spire. But he will be able to venture into the Hassan
II mosque, opened in 1993, a vast neo-Hispanic-cum-Moorish vessel of Taroudant travertine, perched
over the sea, which unites traditional models of Islamic architecture and the latest high-tech advances—
as if the monarch were eager to rival the great mosque of Damascus, of which Al Idrisi would say: "It is
a mosque the likes of which you won't find anywhere in the world, none so beautifully proportioned,
none so stoutly built, none so surely vaulted, none so wonderfully planned, none so admirably decorated
with mosaics and various designs, with enameled tiles and polished marble."[4]

The mosque. Every Friday, the Muslim community listens to the sermon preached from a lofty pulpit, the minbar; *on other days, as here, the faithful carry out their special devotions in the great prayer room facing Mecca and the niche of the mihrab.*

THE KING

IN THE NAME OF ALLAH
AND THE DESCENDANTS OF THE PROPHET

The sultan of Morocco, the *agellid* in Berber, is al-malik, the king, symbol of national unity, responsible for the temporal administration of his subjects and commander in chief of the armed forces. But he is also al-khalifa, the *caliph*, the "successor" descended from the Prophet and al-imam, the guide, the "commander of the faithful" and the "defender of the faith."[1]

Since Abu Bakr, companion and relative of the Prophet, was appointed Khalifat rasul Allah in 632, after consultation by those close to Mahomet who had vowed to obey him, during the first *bay'a* of Islam, caliphal sovereignty has been sacred and imbued with *baraka*, for it has its source in the mission entrusted to the Prophet and to the "gilded chain" of his descendants by God himself. If the king of Morocco is at once caliph and *amir* of the faithful, this—due to this linkage and as specified by the text of the *bay'a* of Oued-ed-Dahab of August 14, 1979—is because the prophet said: "The sultan is like the shadow of God and the Prophet on earth," he reigns in their name, in the way a "Lieutenant" or "Curate" would.[2]

The king has a "two-headed organization," as Mohamed Tozi notes, "made up of a traditional *Makhzen* and a modern administration. He is also a sultan, the patriarch of a large family which extends to all the inhabitants of the *mechouar* of his various palaces, servants, former slaves, *mokhzani*... all those living in areas in close physical proximity. This 'family' relationship applies symbolically to all his Moroccan subjects, those whom the king himself calls 'my family great and small.' "[3] From the Dar-al-Makhzen, the palace, the sultan acts as head of the royal household, guardian of the *qa'ida*, the etiquette and protocol that govern the whole land.

In the late 19th century, his time was organized as follows: "On Fridays," wrote Henri La Martinière in 1884, "he went to the Imperial Mosque which, in each residence at Fez, Meknes, Rabat and Marrakech, lay inside the *casbah*; on Saturdays, in fine weather, before the great heat of summer, he went on a long outing in the environs with the viziers, the procession escorted by mounted detachments [...]. Sunday was set aside for the government cabinet. On Mondays there was an artillery and cannon firing session, of which Mawlay el Hassan was particularly fond; on Tuesdays—an auspicious day in the eyes of Moroccans—people remained indoors, to the great joy of the people of the Court who had a day of rest; on Wednesdays, the sultan inspected the army; on Thursdays, the harem was taken for a walk in the garden of the Aguedal, where the great pool boasted a steam-driven or Menara boat, or alternatively in the famed garden of Redhouane when the king was in Marrakech,"[4] Essentially, the sultan's life was carried on within the Dar-al-Makhzen, well removed from his subjects. The ubiquity of his picture, since the struggle for independence embodied by Mohamed V, on the walls of the tiniest shop with its dim neon

Muhammad VI. Portraits of His Majesty are a pledge of allegiance to the king's person and his family—it is quite common to see depicted beside the sovereign the sister of the deceased king or his younger brother—and a demonstration of the "family" closeness of the Alawite monarchy.

light at the palace entrance, in every possible circumstance of his reign and in every imaginable attire, did not whittle down this distance inherited from the Byzantine model, which was based on the quasi-invisibility of the monarch. It merely shows this remarkable proximity of the benevolent "head of the family" combined with the *haïba*, the reverential fear inspired by the Sherifian sovereign as *amir al-mouminine*, commander of the faithful.

The sultan appears at the gate of his palace in an unchanging setting that symbolizes the permanence of the caliphal institution: the Makhzenian parasol ("of gold-embroidered red velvet" (Walter Harris) ,[5] "red above and compartmented. Red and green underneath" (Delacroix); swathed in the white muslin garment, the *ksa* of finest silk which, in Loti's eyes, made Abd er Rahmane "...akin to a great ghost, in vaporous shrouds;"[6] wearing on his head the red cap, called the *Amama*, covered at the side with a white band; perched on the caliph's white horse, surrounded by a mounted escort, the horses held by the gigantic grooms and followed by the carriage, a gilded kitsch Victorian stand-in for the old imperial chariot, and by the royal procession flanked by a brass band with trumpets and drums in pride of place. And the crowd cries in greeting: "*Allah ibarek fi amer Sidi!*"—May God bless the life of the sultan!

Running counter to this timeless image, at the end of his book on the Sherifian monarchy, Mohamed Tozi describes how one day, not far from the Lyautey Lycée in Casablanca, while reading the headlines of a weekly magazine which ran: " 'Monarchy and modernity: how will tomorrow's institutions be?' " and was illustrated by a photo of Mohamed VI on jet skis, taken when he was still heir to the throne, (a) child walked up to me, eyes glinting with mischief. He said to me in Casablancan slang: " '*Wa'er al malik dial-na*,' which translates loosely as 'Our king's got class, he's cool.' "

Of the various symbols of the Sherifian monarchy, the crown appears on many backgrounds, from the sides of Royal Air Maroc aircraft to city entrances built in honor of the monarch's visit. But it doesn't apppear on the national flag created in 1915 by a *dahir* of Mawlay Yusuf—the red of the sherifs of Mecca and Solomon's seal, symbol of wisdom, its five green branches star-like in the center.

Beneath the makhzen *parasol immortalized by Delacroix, clad in his white silk ksa, and surrounded by his black guard, the king on Bay'a day, the allegiance ceremony of the king's subjects', which brings the country's notables together each year within the palace walls.*

HASSANE TOWER

AN ALMOHAD MOSQUE, SANCTUARY OF ALAWITE MOROCCO

The Hassane Tower esplanade (named after either its architect, a locality, or the owner of the land), tomb of the unknown soldier and mausoleum of the creator of modern Morocco and his son, is the symbolic sanctuary of the Sharif kingdom in Rabat, along with the *kouba* of Mawlay Idriss al Akbar in Fez. All the ingredients of the supreme place are brought together here: an urban hill looking down on a river (the estuary of the Bou Regreg); the ocean in the distance and a fortified city (Sala) below, on the other bank, are the holy mountains; an ancient foundation established by the Almoravids in the late 9th century; a 12th-century sovereign builder, the Almohad Yakub al-Mansur, of whom it is said that: "in his life there was never a moment when he was not having some palace restored, or founding some city;"[1] who, after a resounding victory at Alarcos in July 1196, decided to complete the fortifications of the old military encampment which he called Ribat al-Fath (The Camp of Victory), and embarked on the construction of a mosque which was intended to be the largest in Islam after the Samarra mosque in Iraq. In the modern age, the esplanade is a "place of memory" associated with one of the key moments of the restoration of the political and religious powers of the Alawite monarchy, and the mausoleum of Mohammed V who brought the nationalist cult and the caliphal cult together. To this list we should add a permanent guard made up of sentries in uniforms, immortalized by family snaps.

The tower was first used as a rallying point for the Almohad troops at war with the Berghouata[2] tribes, then, under sultan Abd al Mumin ibn Ali, in the mid-12th century, a rear base for the reconquest of the old empire in Al-Andalus territory. It was here, in 1197, that Yakub decided to build the mosque of his future capital. The year before, as a sign of victory, he had likewise started work on the Giralda of Seville on the model of the Koutoubia. To achieve this as soon as possible, and keep a close eye on the work on his new city, he resided on the spot from April to September, surrounded by artists and craftsmen brought in from all over. In just a few years, the city became, as Leo Africanus noted: "One of the noblest cities of Africa."[3] The mosque was meant to outmatch everything Islam had erected, but without abandoning the decorative rigor and architectural simplicity that had represented the strength of the Almohad reform. The building would measure 600' x 460', its hypostyle hall would boast 312 columns and 42 marble pillars, forming 21 naves, divided into 18 spans flanked by side porticos.

Its minaret would rise to between 210' and 265' with a lantern that sailors could make out from miles around. Its proportions—a square 53' x 53'—were larger than the Koutoubia (39') and the Giralda of Seville (46'). It was designed like the minaret of Kairouan on the model of the north tower of the Great Mosque of Damascus (early 8th century). Its inner area (which was halted at a height of 145') had a ramp wide enough to allow a horse to reach its summit through a series of six vaulted halls. Its sides, all

With its gigantic proportions, its oceanside site, and its kinship with the Giralda of Seville and the Koutoubia of Marrakech, the Hassane tower from Rabat bedazzles onlookers with the last lights of imperial Morocco. Moroccans happily meet here to be photographed alongside top model sentries.

different, were divided into three levels embellished with arcatures and tracery carved in the red stone walls. All works ground to a halt at the death of Yakub in 1199 and neither minaret nor mosque were ever completed. Thirteen years later, the defeat of Las Navas de Tolosa[4] crushed any hope of reconquering the Almohad empire. In 1260, Rabat was occupied by the Spanish. In 1500, when Leo Africanus visited the city, he observed: "Rabat is a large city built in modern times by Mansur, king and pontiff of Marrakech. Since the death of Mansur, this city has started to wane....Today, Rabat is in a worse state than ever. I think you would scarcely find 100 inhabited houses in it, near the citadel, with a few little shops." In 1755, what remained of the mosque was destroyed by the earthquake that flattened Lisbon, 500 miles to the north.

On March 9, 1956, almost a year after his triumphant return to Morocco, the site Mohammed V selected for the Friday sermon was indeed a center of imperial Morocco of bygone times. "By choosing the unfinished 12th-century monument," wrote Charles-André Julien, "he [Mohammed V] revived the tradition of the glorious—and pious—Almohads. The call on March 7 may have issued from the caliph, setting forth its temporal policies, but that of the Hassane Tower, on the 9th, came from the imam who addressed not only Muslim Moroccans, but also the community of the prophet (ummat al-mahi), and all those who professed the Islamic faith, and fellow nations. Surrounded by dignitaries, wearing the traditional djellaba in the midst of a throng of 15,000 believers, he really did come across like the 'real emir of the faithful, of all the faithful in the Islamic world.' "[5] In 1971, when the mausoleum of Mohammed V was completed in accordance with the canons of the architectural and artisanal tradition of the master craftsmen, the *bouallem* of Morocco (even though it was the work of a Vietnamese architect, Vo Tuan), the most visited *kouba* in Morocco was created. Mawlay Abdallah, a younger son of Mohammed V, and Hassan II would join him at rest in 1983 and 1999 respectively, in the holy of holies of the Alawite monarchy.

Rabat: the mausoleum of Muhammed V. Opposite the Hassane tower, the mausoleum of the creator of modern Morocco, together with Mawlay Abdallah and Hassan II. Designed by the Vietnamese architect Vo Tuan and built by Moroccan master-craftsmen, it is a fine, albeit slightly cautious, example of the revival of the classical architectural tradition of the early 1970s.

THE KOUBA

HOUSE OF HOLINESS

This is a hallmark of the Moroccan landscape, its trademark and most consistent counterpoint in an ocean of geographical differences. This small structure, always cube shaped, is surmounted by a *kouba*, the dome after which it is named. The *kouba* is the tomb of a holy figure such as you might meet on the roads of Morocco.

A single door leads to its one room, which is dimly lit by small windows. Sometimes there is an adjoining outbuilding and a wall built by the entrance. The most important examples are linked with buildings of the *zaouïa*, which venerates the buried holy man. In most cases, however, the kouba stands alone, on top of a hill or by a road or tree, or with nothing around it, visible from miles away against the blue sky. In Morocco, the top of the cube is bare or adorned with crenelated merlons, or alternatively ringed by a hem of ceramics. The dome may at times be hidden by the four sloping sides of a green-tiled roof. The white walls are sometimes covered with handprints of liquid henna—a substitute for sacrificial blood.

The hemispherical shape of the dome symbolizes the celestial vault set above the earth, mind and body. The kouba are located in isolated spots, visible from afar. Émile Dermenghem notes that holy men "dislike competition"[1] and would be annoyed that a more beautiful tomb might steal their top billing and divert offerings. The interior of the funerary room is usually one room with bare walls punctuated by three niches. The clay floor is covered with a mat, on which the *qbar* stands. In the most popular sanctuaries, the tomb is covered with embroidered fabric. The place can't be compared with a mosque; it is "the house of holiness," the place where people worship a *marabout*, a wise man, and where they expect, in return, the beneficial effects of his *baraka*. [2]

"The tomb sparkled on the reddish hillside" (J. and J.M.G. Le Clezio, Gens de nuages): *the kouba are solitary monuments where the local saint buried is venerated—hub of traditional festivals and the magic square in the Moroccan countryside.*

THE CAFÉ

MEN'S TURF

Coffee, according to various authors, is "always bad" in Morocco, and should only be sampled, "for the record, no more."[1]

It is true, Morocco isn't a coffee country. *Yemeni mocha*, which has been usurped by mint tea, only holds sway close to the Algerian border in towns and cities affected by Ottoman influences, like Oujda and Taroudant, where it is drunk spiced with pepper, with a cardamom pod, cinnamon, a clove and ginger. We also find it in the coastal ports which were once under Portuguese and Spanish rule.

Everywhere else, tea reigns supreme—in places where people used to drink sickly sweet infusions of mint and absinthe, which immediately quenched thirsts. But if you should happen to be served a coffee "boiled after infusion and made vaguely Turkish-style with too much sugar"[2] or, worse still, in the south, a "café cassé," freeze-dried and sprinkled with powdered milk, Moroccan coffee is not quite as bad as people say. But we are not concerned with coffee here as much as cafés, symbols of Moroccan city life where you can sometimes order everything but coffee. The café isn't easy to pinpoint on the Moroccan imaginary map, for it is a place with no precise definition: "Just as prolific as the mosque," notes Omar Carlier, "attuned, like the latter, to prayer times, but just as much to transport and office timetables too, to market activities, the fluctuations of skies and seasons, the destitution of the jobless and the relaxation of passers-by, is it not open to one and all (or rather to all men) at any time?"[3] What does a Moorish café in Figuig or Tangier, and a grand café in Casa have in common? What do a Barbary café close to the mosque, the grand colonnaded café in Casa, and a punters' betting café for regulars have in common? How is it possible to bring together, under the same banner, the "Zrireh" blue café of Edmond Amran El-Maleh in Essaouira with its clay floor and its low light ,[4] and the "La falaise" Hala café described by Paul Bowles in Tangier, at the mercy of the elements and surveying the Strait of Gibraltar with its matted terraces and kif-smokers? We can gauge its complexity by the works of writers, as in Tangier, city of cafés.

What would *le pain nu* (naked bread) be without the Si Moh Café, the Zagora Café, the Normandy, the Jacobito, or the Café Central? Without the Roxy, or Dean's Bar? What would Gysin's "devouring desert" be without the terrace of the Café de Paris? What would Tangier be without the cafés of the Chico Socco, where the shadowy figure of those writers who have drunk a Flag-Pils there, while listening to Nat King Cole, still roam? But also, as Paul Bowles notes, those "who have been washed up here as a last resort, at the end of their tether, waiting for work, or a check or a visa or a residence permit, which they'll never get."

People in cafés usually drink mint tea and spend the day talking. The café is an irreplaceable observation post, and a permanent forum.
It also stands in for the office, and serves as courtroom, recruitment agency and post office—a place loved by writers.

THE HOUSE

FAMILY CITADEL

Houses built of rough earth in the High Atlas, whitewashed cottages in the countryside around Fez, bluish cubes of the Oudaias in Rabat, monumental *dar* in the imperial cities, invisible and delightful *riyad* in Marrakech, adobe forts in the Draa and Dades valleys—there are as many Moroccan houses as there are climatic regions, economies and lifestyles. But the traditional dwelling still has a consistency and a coherence recognized all over the country.

In 1683, Germain Mouette described the city home: "The houses of both Fezes, as well as those of the other cities of Barbary, are built square and covered with a terrace. The walls, which lead to the streets or neighbors have no openings; they usually have four low bedrooms, 8' to 10' wide and 25' to 30' long, some larger, some smaller. The doors of these bedrooms in the middle, and daylight comes in through slits, reaching both ends of each room. The court is at the center, where there is usually a well, or, if the residence is a wealthy one, there are shell-shaped pools which gush water, and the occasional fishpond, hemmed by orange and lemon trees, laden with fruit all year round."[1] The traditional house is based on a small number of invariable features which still exist despite recent changes.

The visitor venturing for the first time into the medina of a large city, who strays from the *souks* in search of the "Arab city," will be impressed by the bare walls of the houses, their narrow doors, and the virtual absence of any opening onto the street. He has so often heard of "Muslim imprisonment" that he scarcely registers any surprise, but the sensation of walking through a closely observed area never leaves him. The house itself seems to have vanished behind a screen. Its facade is just a wall punctuated by a door that seems altogether anonymous. The facade is often no wider than the door. Nothing sets it apart from the wall that forms the local cul-de-sac or lane, the derb, with which it blends completely. Like the medina, it has no outside prospect—designed as a series of impenetrable obstacles and zigzagging routes. A more educated eye may pick up the subtle signs transmitted by the entrance, but it will not be able to get any precise idea of the scale of the abode. The onlooker will not know whether it is something splendid or in ruins. "Outside, there is nothing," writes Jean Gallotti, author of a book written in the period of the Protectorate about the houses of Morocco, "bare walls, flat, windowless and hostile. Here and there a loophole or a slit or a tiny window bared by a wooden lattice."[2] This is the image of the Moroccan house: an urban stronghold hermetically sealed, which shows nothing at all to the outside world. The protective enclosure around the family and its corollary, the imprisonment of women, are still the decisive factor. The public image of the house has nothing to do with its facade, and plenty to do with this respect for the inviolable frontier which encircles the woman. Most authors point to the ancestral identification of the house and home with woman (and thus with family), defined equally by the same word—dar—and recurring in the expression: "How's your house? (otherwise

The Moroccan home likes to give itself the look of a citadel. Its walls boast few windows and its door is usually double-locked.
Its face only smiles on guests. But no sooner has its threshold been crossed than it becomes the most generous of hostesses.

put, your wife). Everything all right? May God be praised!" This kind of defensive apparatus is also the expression of the principles of the Koran which thus controls access to the home: "O ye believers! Do not enter any abodes other than your own before seeking admission and having greeted those within it! Tell believers to lower their gaze and be chaste. It will be more decent for them. When you enter abodes, hail one another mutually with a greeting from Allah, the blessed, the excellent."[3]

The threshold, or doorway—the atba—is one of the most fascinating places of the Moroccan home. It has several functions. If a house is properly lived in, people say that "it has a good threshold," but this also means that the doorway must never be forced. Whatever happens, you must never cross the threshold in an untimely or overly direct way. This would be likened to an infringement of the horma—the sacred area which is both defended and venerated, and separates the outside world and the home, and at the same time unites them.

The bride crosses the threshold for the first time on the back of a relative. This way her persence in her new household will not ruffle the old order of things because she hasn't stepped on the home's threshold, it's as if she hadn't entered the home at all. It is also possible to interpret this tradition in a different way: to prevent the young bride from bringing evil spirits from the outside world with her, the members of her new household act as if she had never left....[4] F. Légey observes that the act of entering a new abode requires that a girl or boy should cross the threshold first, so as not to disturb the jnoun any more than necessary. It is worth noting that most of the premises given over to services are traditionally located close to the street, when they are not grouped around a dar al-khdam, a service house on the first floor where guests are often housed. The real house is as far as possible from the street. It is customary to spread out the visitor's expectations, and proceed in stages. The zigzagging route that leads to the center of the house—the setwan—is not merely designed to ward off prying eyes; it is also designed to postpone the entrance to the holy of holies, and leave the outside world and all its disorderly bustle behind you by disorienting the visitor's evil spirits.

Opposite: *The center of the house, the room where people congregate, encapsulates all its wealth: zelliges everywhere, stucco carved with arabesques, sculpted, painted wood, niches decorated like the mihrab in the mosque, chandeliers, benches, embroidered fabrics and furniture that is moved about as the day dictates.*

Following pages: *The rooms of the house adjoin the patio by way of large wooden doors. People spend time in and outside the house depending on the moment, the season and the moving boundaries that crisscross the family space.*

The Patio

THE HOME'S SQUARE

Once over the threshold of the house and through the doors separating it from the west *ed-dar*, the visitor leaves the outside world behind. The narrow street suddenly swells, the colorless outside world opens on to a shimmering rectangle covered with ceramics, carved and painted wood and sculpted plaster; heat gives way to the coolness of a fountain; a beautiful golden light pours over the courtyard; the bare facade is forgotten, as is the din of the souk; there are decorations everywhere; symmetry is king. The sky, which almost vanishes from the street appears again in the form of a large square bound by beautiful blue-green tiles reflected in the *zelliges* and the mirroring surface of the fountain.

No travel writing nor any study of the Moroccan home ever omits this bedazzlement: "When you've bent low," writes Jean Gallotti, "to pass through the door of a house and when you've groped your way down a dark corridor, you experience astonishment at suddenly seeing the sun shimmering on the orange trees and the flowering almonds, among the colonnades, the mosaic paths, the painted doors and shutters, the blue balustrades and slats. Everything is clarity, color, order, fresh and clean. Far from feeling like recoiling, as when you see those pit-like *dar*, you are drawn by a powerful spell. It doesn't seem like you're coming in, but, on the contrary, like you're going out. The prison, the dark dungeon, uncomfortable and stifling, is the street you've just left. And you're seized by a desire to live in this enclosed garden, where the twofold freedom of the eyes, which can see, and the mind, which can dream, has taken refuge."[1] André Chevrillon described the Bennis House, where he was received in Fez in 1905, in this way: after the narrow maze of streets in old Fez, he saw opening before him "...the secret beauties of a large Moorish house: lofty arcades around a spacious rectangle, and, right in the middle, a basin spouting water. Behind the pillars there appeared powerful cedar doors where old geometric arabesques intertwined their triangles. But one side of this patio is not quite closed off; beyond, framed by a double portico, gardens withdraw...."[2]

The courtyard, as Loti remarks, is "...the wonder of the home." In the house where the French embassy is installed in Fez, it has "a floor of mosaics, where thousands of small designs in blue, yellow, black and white sparkle and glisten; all around, a series of Moorish arcades festooned with filigree and, on the upper floor, above these arches and stone arabesques, a gallery made of cedar wood with ornamental openings."[3] Its main embellishment is the fountain which fills the middle or may in some cases be set against a wall. Everything in the courtyard converges on this feature, with its cool, splashing water. Going into a patio on a summer's day after wandering through the searing heat of the *medina*, hearing its music echo off the walls of the house, and breathing in the mist of the cool gushing water flowing over the painted blue fountain is one of the pleasures of the Moroccan home.

But the patio isn't designed solely for this rapture. It is the hub of home life. Its role is similar to a pub-

Paradise. A tree or two, a pond and a fountain basin turn the patio into a garden and the dar into a riyad. But there must also be a rich floor of zelliges, and more zelliges on the walls and columns, panels of ceramics, carved lintels and the great square of the sky above.

lic square, designed only for private use. As Kaddour Zouilai observes it is "... a small exterior recreated in the hollow of the interior."[4] The space of the courtyard or patio is governed by the code of the *aila*, the patriarchal family, and is the center of an endless negotiation. Many descriptions emphasize its ambivalence. The patio is a living area but also a place of passage and obligatory meetings. It is a plentifully decorated theatre as well, and a crucial functional center. Fatima Mernissi has beautifully described the ways and customs, in the mid-20th century, of a large *Fassi* residence. Every morning, as a child, the author waited on the threshold that separated her parents' living room from the patio for her mother to awaken before being allowed to meet up with her cousins who, since the parents were up, were permitted to play there. In any event, she noted: "It was never possible to really have fun in the courtyard, it was too public."[5]

The patio is neither a playground nor an outdoor living room, but a bit of both, encompassing too many different functions (washing things, getting meals ready, henna sessions, laundry, embroidery, removing the dust from carpets and blankets etc.), for someone not to be always keeping a close eye on it. The symmetry of the rooms giving on to the courtyard through huge doors was designed not only to guarantee the house's architectural harmony, but also to distribute the symbolic areas of the different family members evenly. A fairness that is often challenged!

The real dar is the great patriarchal house around its courtyard; the mansions of the austere middle-class families of Fez with their galleries on several floors, playing with the contrasts between varnished zelliges and matt whitewash, dazzling color and dark cedar lintels.

THE TERRACE

WOMEN'S REALM

When the stairway reaches the terrace it grows more narrow, just like the door that leads to the upper part of the house. As the exclusive realm of women and children, the *stah*, or terrace, long ago abandoned the privileges of the harem. But it has lost none of its fascination. Men were only allowed there on certain occasions, otherwise their presence was inappropriate. In an orientalist scene, straight out of *The Thousand and One Nights*, Loti has described the terrace life of Fez at the end of the 19th century: "They go about in groups, these women, or else they sit and chat on the walls, their legs dangling over the courtyards and streets; or they stretch out, nonchalant and prone, with their arms beneath the nape of their necks. From one house to the next, they clamber to visit one another, sometimes using short ladders, or planks making do as bridges.... Whether mistress or slave, casting caste differences to the winds, they walk about any old way, laughing together and often clasping one another with a semblance of complete equality."[1] The kindness and concern of the other, the *hanan* may hold sway on the lower floors, but the terrace is where there is the greatest freedom. "Playing hide-and-seek in the olive jars," writes Fatima Mernissi, "wasn't the only activity allowed on the terrace. Grown-ups committed far more serious crimes, like chewing gum, varnishing their fingernails and smoking cigarettes." As for looking at the girls next door,that, adds F. Mernissi, "was a real sin, a dangerous infringement of the *hudud*."[2] Despite these bans, the terrace is often the stage for first loves; people arrange to take tea on the terrace of a summer eve, and then sleep up there.

In low-rent housing blocks, these traditional customs give way to all sorts of functions: chickens and rabbits are reared on terraces, and a sheep will be taken up there before being slaughtered. Usually, the wash house and the hanging laundry take up most of the space. It's also on the terrace that major cooking preparations are undertaken when important guests are expected. Wool and seeds are dried there, too, as are tomatoes, apricots and peppers. It is quite common to build the bedroom for an elder son there, or the *gorfa*, the upper room for the master of the house. Men have their pigeons and doves up there and sometimes they set up actual garages amid the plants grown by another family member.

In town, the terrace that has a gorfa turns the roof of this uppermost part of the home into another terrace, reached via a ladder, from where there are sweeping views over the neighborhood. It was up to this "forbidden terrace" that harem women, suffering from *hem*—a slight depression—climbed "to find the peace and quiet and the beauty that they needed."[3]

The terrace, realm of women, is a place that is both secret and open, a place of observation and a place of withdrawal; a territory where prohibitions are eased a little by the hosts' games and confabs or secret meetings. The way the terrace has recently developed is whittling away this age-old privilege.

THE RIYAD

A PRIVATE PARADISE

Of all the many types of gardens in Morocco, few cast such a powerful spell as the *riyad*. Unlike the *hadika*, the public garden, and the *jnan*, the open orchard, or even the *arsa* or vegetable garden, the riyad is a private pleasure garden either adjoining or in the middle of the house, and enclosed on all sides. It comes in a stunning array of forms: "There is," writes Malek Chebel, "the palace-garden, the actual palace of the garden, the fountain-garden, the patio-garden, and the garden of profusion, which is a kind of virgin forest where the mind may stray."[1] Among the most luxurious of gardens, the riyad is adorned with a gazebo, a *menzeh*, with its main room, and the *gorfa*, from where guests can view the garden paths from a covered terrace, like a miniature landscape.

There are three main versions of the riyad in Morocco: the first is the rectangular garden with cross-shaped walks surrounded on all four sides by the dwelling. The second, more akin to the classical definition, appoints the house, the main body of which extends in two wings over an oblong and enclosed garden which in turn extends its paths beyond the dwelling as far as a pavilion, preceded by a portico and flanked by a loggia. The third variety juxtaposes the house and the garden in relation to the narrowness of the plot, based on a staggered plan or a set of terraces, as in the heights of the Fez *medina*. There are actually countless relationships between a riyad and the home.

There are some who believe these gardens come straight from the *Alhambra* or the *Generalife*, and the *crucero*, the cross-shaped gardens of Seville. Yet, with their delicate pavilions and rosebeds, they also suggest Persian or Moghul origins. Archaeologists have been looking for their origins in Mesopotamia, among the gardens of Suse, Ctesiphon, Nineveh and Babylon. Some think they see a remote replica of the enclosed gardens of Egypt, with their clever irrigation systems and ponds, imported by the Berbers; a legacy of Carthage, or a transcribed version of the famous garden of the Cretan palace of Alcinous, praised by Ulysses. For historians of Africa under the Romans, there is no doubt: the Roman villa, with its atrium and its porticoed patio, is its direct model, as in Volubilis. For others, it was imported from Al-Andalus in the time of the Umayyads, after gaining a firm foothold in Baghdad, Damascus and Kairouan. Recent excavations have unearthed 12th-century riyad in Marrakech, Chichaoua and Belyounech. Its basic layout, worked out 4,000 years BCE, on the banks of the Euphrates, involves a four-part division around the cosmic mountain, loftier than the Himalayas, symbolized by the central fountain, and the *qanat* which holy writings compare to the rivers of paradise, a celestial replica of the four great rivers of the known world: Tigris, Euphrates, Nile and Ganges.

It is in that garden of bliss—haunt of *houris*, those beautiful dark-eyed virgins, and handsome *ephebi*—that the anti-desert was developed in Andalusia from the early days of the conquest. But there would

Its current vogue shows up the paradoxes of privacy. Scaled to the human body, the riyad is also a miniature palace.

66   *In the eyes of its new owner, the merest quadrilateral can turn into a palace courtyard; and its meagre plantlife and decoration into wild luxuriance.*

be no attempt to carry on the chaos of its vegetation—bitter orange and orange trees, bananas, figs, pomegranates and palms in profusion. The rigor of the general design of its walks and the art of the *zel-liges* and the stucco and wooden carvings covering every surface, gave it the geometric mirror and the calligraphic script of the *dhikr*, the mystical prayer that befits the garden of paradise.

Sultans didn't develop only a small taste for the riyad, sometimes it was of monumental proportions as in the Al-Badi palace in Marrakech. Near their palaces they planted huge orchards encircled by walls encompassing, in the age of the Almohads, as many as a thousand acres, with enormous *aguedal*, ponds at times embellished with a central island, as in Marrakech and Meknes. Similarly, in the city of Mawlay Ismail, we find the pond measuring 1,115' x 485', built within the *mechouar*, and fed by the "house with ten *norias*," or the aguedal of Marrakech, built in the 12th century to the south of the city. Destroyed in the 17th century, it was then rebuilt in 1830, under the reign of Mawlay Abd al-Rahman, within its present-day walls. And there is the garden of the Menara with its square pond inhabited by big carps, its huge olive grove and its timeless pavilion standing beside the mirror-like expanse of water.

A stroll around the garden is essential for the visitor, enabling her to view the extent of the sultan's wealth and the order imposed upon his grounds. The contrast between the world of the riyad and the world of the street must be total. To create this paradisiacal effect, there's no need to have the garden covering vast expanses—its visible boundaries are a reminder that is part of a complete and perfect world. The riyad es-sghir of the Bahia palace, completed in 1898, is known as the "blessed garden" because of its cozy proportions unlike the "great riyad." If all it takes is a few orange trees, a cypress strung with bougainvillea and wisteria, and four palms to turn the courtyard of a dar into a riyad, this is because in the land of Islam the garden is first and foremost a notion. It is that possibility of projecting in the imaginary, based on a handful of essential factors, a paradise said by the various writings, to reside in seventh heaven, "close to the outermost jujube tree," where the prophet made a stop on his night journey in a nowhere land called the "non-where."[2]

*"The symmetry, the cleanliness, the wonderful arrangement of the trees, the abundance and variety
of the fruit from a thousand unknown species, their freshness, their beauty, everything delighted my eye."*

The garden of The Thousand and One Nights *is not a dream, but a faithful mirror of the divine world.*

THE DESERT

SENTINEL OF ELUSIVE ORIGIN

From the edge of Western Sahara to the Grand Erg on the Algerian border, along the length of the Atlas Mountains, Morocco follows the gilded rim of the desert. Tourists are all too aware of this, since the mighty wilderness of southern Algeria has been closed: first thing in the morning, convoys of four-wheel drive vehicles start out from Erfoud, taking the Merzouga road, and head for the miniature Erg Chebbi desert, just beyond the parking lot. Then they return in the afternoon, rewarded by a few digitized square miles of sand.

Those who venture from Oujda to Figuig, or take the road to Tamegroute, Tagounite and M'Hamid, are relatively few and far between. Only a handful ever get to Smara, the holy city of Cheikh Ma al-Aïnin, via the Tan-Tan, Tindouf and Laayoune tracks, peppered with military checkpoints.

But when they stop beside a palm grove or a *ksar*, heads full of images of oases, camels, tents fit for caïds, and "blue men," they are already in the heart of the desert. The dream doesn't always meet expectations, but it doesn't really matter. The desert is a land of mirages, you don't need to sacrifice your life to it, eyes trained on a hopping jerboa, like Théodor Monod, or take it on bare-handed like Wilfred Thesiger, to be spellbound by it. Pictures say it all quite well, it just takes a few dunes and, as the poster puts it, "The desert is all yours."

It's probably not quite the sandy desert of Egypt, the Ténéré, the Tassili, or the Namib, nor is it the mythical *bled el-khouf*, land of fear, or the *bled es-sif*, land of the sword, but an invitation to press on a bit further, with the promise of a return—a taste of vastness. Some are a bit disappointed that so often you have to cross stony plateaus before getting to the "real desert," which they want to be just like the desert in "Fort Saganne"[1] or "Djebel Amour."[2]

We'll discuss meeting the Beni Kelboun a little later—those dog-headed men so feared by geographers in the Middle Ages. Looking at the Sijilmassa ruins, we shall just imagine the great nomad caravans plying the gold routes and the slave routes which, in the 8th century, had established one of the crossroad cities of the Maghreb between sub-Saharan Africa and the land of the setting sun. And we'll lovingly retain the image of those Aït Mribel, the tent people, who we thought we might have encountered in the "blue men" offering to be our guide.

We are frequently reminded that many great Berber dynasties hail from the desert: the Almoravids in the 11th century came from the banks of the Senegal river via Sijilmassa and Taroudant, descending the slopes of the High Atlas to found Marrakech before reconquering the former reaches of the Umayyad empire in Al-Andalus; the Merinids, a Zenata tribe, hailed from the upland plateaus of the Saharan Atlas; the Saadians in the 16th century emerged from the Draa valley, and the Alawites, in the 17th cen-

Unlike Algeria and Tunisia, Morocco doesn't have one large expanse of desert, but rather numerous "gateways to the desert," sweeping stony plateaus and sandy wastes that remind travelers of those sailors of the sands from the past.

tury, issued from the sands of Tafilalet, not far from Erfoud and Rissani. Islam turned the desert into a vehicle of its expansion, where all roads to Mecca had to pass. In it, the Moroccan dynasties retained the nomadic reputation of the Deep South—the Grand Sud—even in Andalusia. But on their rush northward, they often forgot to ensure their power over a land on which they had, with no regrets, turned their back, a land which would dodge their control for many years. The desert is Morocco's back country, its hinterland, but it is also the flipside of the paradise of Islam, the Ras el Madajba, the origin of solitude, a territory abandoned by God. As Jémia and J.M.G. Le Clézio observe: "The Sahara is not merely the beauty of dusks, the sensual undulating dunes, the mirage caravans. It is also a land where the standard of living is among the world's lowest, and where infant mortality is the highest (35 per 1000, as opposed to less than 1 per 1000 in the industrialized countries). Where well water is bitter; where people delight in sweeter rain water."[3] And where trachoma is still rife.

For the western imagination, the Moroccan desert is not so much a country, as a major route to the edge of the *Maghreb*, and then to sub-Saharan Africa.

The goal of those first 19th-century explorers—Major Laing in 1827, and the cobbler René Caillié in 1828—was Timbuktu, that legendary city described as the capital of gold. Gerhard Rohlfs set out in the 1860s in search of Sudan and Guinea, and stayed for an entire year in Ouezzan, only because the Sherif Sidi al-Hadj Abd es-Seam persuaded him to. In 1879, doctor Oscar Lenz departed on a reconnaissance trip to the Atlas, and also ended up in Timbuktu. Charles de Foucauld, who explored Saharan Morocco in 1883, had another goal in mind, to provide the still uncharted land with the most accurate geographical description possible, with a view to its imminent conquest. A few years later his reasons were quite different—his conquest was mystical.

At the end of her life, in 1904, Isabelle Eberhardt went to Figuig, Oujda and Aïn Sefra, but her purpose was less to explore than to blend even more deeply into the Muslim world. Odette du Puigaudeau and Marion Sénones also experienced "the call of the desert," in the 1930s, and then again in 1950, but traveling was aimed at tourists: "at those with enough leisure and passion to go on discovering things."[4]

The blue men. Desert people, perforce impassive and impenetrable, heirs to all the world's nobility,
like these blue warriors of Smara, who intrigued many a generation. Reality is more complex,
for they draw on a patchwork of peoples—Tuaregs of Berber origin, black Tubu, Moors and Chleuhs.

THE ATLAS

MOUNTAIN OF MOUNTAINS

Atlas was a giant condemned by Zeus to bear upon his shoulders, arms and head the great vault of the sky, standing waist-deep in the sea. But in ancient geography the Atlas was a vast mountain range, its skyline vague, lying somewhere near the Pillars of Hercules and the Hesperides, the "daughters of night," at the western end of the known world. For Herodotus, the Atlas was "...narrow and round on every side and so high, it is said, that it is impossible to see the peaks, for the clouds never part, either in summer or in winter; the people in these parts say that it is the pillar of the sky."[1] For Pliny the Elder, it was the territory of the Atlantes, vegetarian giants who lived twenty days to the west of Garamantes "in the midst of solitudes," on fearsome borders, "in the very spot where nature ceases."[2]

For a long time, the Atlas was a sacred, holy mountain range, inspiring fear and awe. Its diversity only came to light in modern times. It was not until the 20th century that its "riant valleys" were explored, along with its *ksour* and its flat-roofed adobe villages, hugging the earth's contours, and earth-colored too. These days the Atlas is undergoing a influx of "mountain tourism." There are five different mountain chains crossing Tunisia, Algeria and Morocco from east to west.

The Tell Atlas and the Rif, which survey the Mediterranean for 1000 miles, form the first two ranges. Their peaks are not that high, but they are jagged. They create a fragmented chain, criss-crossed by brief, shady valleys, often creating sharp contrasts. The two great strongholds of the Rif are Chaouen the Berber and Tetouan the Andalusian. The Middle Atlas, which soars over the Moulouya to the east, is a large limestone plateau, lashed by wind and rain for much of the year. It separates Atlantic Morocco from eastern Morocco. Its main centers are Azrou, Khenifra and Sefrou. Like the Rif, the Middle Atlas, home to the Beni Mguild, is a principal center of Berber resistance. The High Atlas is a gigantic battlement, 450 miles long, peopled by the Masmouda and Zenata tribes, running from the Algerian border towards the Atlantic, and separating the Mediterranean from the Sahara. It is higher (its loftiest peak, Mount Toubkal, rising 13,672', is one of many summits in a range that boasts more than a hundred major ones), wider, more verdant and more desert-like than the Middle Atlas, and is called the Adrar-n-dern, the mountain of mountains.

The Anti-Atlas runs parallel to the High Atlas from the ocean to the oued Ziz and the Tafilalet. This is the realm of the sedentary Chleuh Berbers, a kind of mountainous Sahara, home to those *agadirs* or fortified granaries, where harvests are stored.

The Atlas is a realm within a realm. The urgent call for freedom, the pride and the Berber Irredentism of its inhabitants, combined with the wealth and variety of its traditions dating back to the pre-Islamic period, make these mountains one of contemporary Morocco's greatest treasures.

Throughout present-day Morocco, the huge mountain fold that once connected Spain and Morocco in the form of a "Betic bridge" and stretched as far as Sicily, thrusts its soaring stone crags and dizzy peaks skywards, with its terraced houses and earth-hued ksours.

THE DONKEY

LORD AND MASTER

There are said to be six times as many donkeys in Tunisia, with its herd of 170,000, than in Morocco, which comes way behind Egypt with its two million, all pack-saddled. Although they are in the process of being abandoned for less cantankerous vehicles, they are far from vanishing from the Moroccan land-scape. Large cities are relegating them to the outskirts, maybe, but they are there, whenever you care to look, at the roadside, in a *medina* lane, in country *souks*, on a mountain path, on the roof of a house, or on a bridge over a motorway, laden with photogenic bundles of merchandise. They move along in a row, or on their own, ridden side-saddle on colorful layers of fabric. This is an age-old custom, not yet com-pletely forgotten by teenagers riding their scooters with both legs dangling from one side of the saddle. For the Koran, the *behime*—the donkey—like the horse, the mule, the camel, the bee and the household dog, is a useful animal for which thanks must be given to God. Only the evil spirit living in its flanks since Noah's Ark can explain this creature's offhandedness and stubbornness. This is why some *hadith* put a ban on eating its flesh. "If you hear braying," wrote Abu Huraya, "find refuge with God far from Satan, for this donkey has seen the devil." Angels find the donkey's braying unpleasant, and it can quash the prayer, but it is also said to attract rain. Its thighbone keeps husbands drowsy at the timely moment, its tongue prevents it from closing its mouth, and its ear is recommended "...to be like a donkey in its sexu-al relations." The donkey also turns out to be a good model. And when it's wild, it can even bring *bara-ka*. It is said that Mawlay Ismail was most proud of his wild asses from Guinea, and forbade anyone to go near them.

For tourists, the donkey is the messenger of time-honored "millennial Morocco," the symbol of a way of life that has remained the same since the Phoenicians—or was it the Carthaginians?—brought it to the gates of the Gharb. "I am quite dazed," wrote Nancy George in *Marrakech la rouge*, "jostled, pushed by little donkeys trotting straight ahead, laden with two soft baskets, tied with a length of woven reed, full of stones and aloe leaves." As soon as Pierre Loti arrived in Tangier, he saw "...countless little donkeys here replacing trucks and trolleys, which are quite unknown."[1] The caravan that set out to the sultan's cities numbered "a hundred stubborn mules and stupid camels." One of the first cries that assailed the ear of the travelling writer was "Balek! Balek!—Be careful, watch out!" "Balek! Look out!" wrote the poet Adonis." It's lord donkey! He is swathed in the melancholy of childhood, and bowed beneath the weight of all manner of angel: vegetables, fruit, greens."[2]

Morocco is the land of the horse, winged creature of the Prophet and of conquest, and sherif of the Fantasia. But the donkey is its long-suffering companion, its demon of luckless days, and its most loyal servant. It trots along in all our imagery of Morocco.

THE ARGAN TREE

TREE OF THE SOUTH

Postcards of Mawlay al-Hassan in Essaouira, just opposite the Café de France, beneath the spruce trees Edmond Amran El Maleh was so fond of, have long made this tree their fetish image. The argan tree is the national tree. It is majestic, immense like a giant olive, and the hanging pasture of those adventurous goats of southwest Morocco—a veritable blessing when there's nothing else growing on the horizon. During a "skillful hunt" in the vicinity of Agadir, Ernst Jünger observed, "On the track, tree-climbing goats, a species peculiar to Morocco. They clamber high up into the branches and graze on the leaves. Hint of some Darwinian transition."[1]

You'll find the argan tree on the coast road with its overhead cargo and attendant goatherd, alert for the inevitable photograph, for which he'll ask a high fee. Its landscape is like a vast garden of paradise. But no gardener ever actually planned it. "Despite the spacing of the trees, giving it the look of an olive orchard," writes Louis Emberger, "the argan grove must be regarded as a forest and not as an orchard, for it has strictly natural origins. No human being has ever planted, grafted, propagated or tended an argan tree."[2]

The overlord of this natural wonder bears the learned Linnaean name of *Argania sideroxylon*, so-called for its timber which has a density that is nothing less than astral, and as hard as the metal of an asteroid. It is also known as *Argania spinosa* because of its thorns. Its trunk is rough and tough. It grows from the snowy uplands of the Atlas down to the ocean between Essaouira and Agadir, and works its way up the Draa Valley as far as Tindouf. Its fruit, called sapotes, are the size of large olives. They are coffee-colored and cleft lengthwise by a thin white seam. Their shiny, hard nut contains a kernel which, once grilled and pounded, yields a delicious hazelnut-flavored oil. Argan groves are part of Morocco's state-owned forests. Their production is distributed in accordance with the rules of an age-old entitlement which earmarks the usufruct for the nearest inhabitants.

"The argan tree," writes Mohammed Khaïr-Eddine," is undoubtedly the most typical symbol of this mountainous land, glorified by legend with its myths and its mysteries, which, at the very least, cause an imperceptible knot to form in your stomach when you come upon one of those ageless old men whose wrinkles tell a tale of bloodshed and struggle for survival, interspersed with simple, fleeting joys."[3]

Goats, sheep and camels all have a soft spot for the year-round leaves of the argan tree, which are only shed when new buds sprout.
When conditions become too dry, the argan tree rids itself of its foliage to save its strength.

THE PALM TREE

THE PROPHET'S BLESSED TREE

The palm tree's silhouetted shape may well be part of the most hackneyed exotic imagery—which Victor Segalen recommended be got rid of right away (along with the camel, the colonial helmet and the yellow sun), but it doesn't surrender that easily.

In Morocco there is no way you can avoid what Linnaeus considered amongst "the princes of the plant world," and rightly called "Principes" because of its pride of place. The palm tree shows up everywhere, beside a *oued*, or a stony *kouba*, in the tight enclosure of a *riyad*, lining the avenues of modern cities, and growing in desert sands.

The oldest species of palm is a dwarf variety, Chamaerops humilis, which has thrived in these parts since 6,000 BCE. The most famous species is Phoenix dactylifera, the date palm which the Greeks reckoned had been imported to their territory by the Phoenicians. From Egypt and Mesopotamia it gradually found its way to the shores of the Atlantic Ocean along the caravan route, well before the Phoenicians stowed it in their holds. The Jews are also said to have transplanted the seeds of dates marked by Solomon's seal. But it is because of Islam that the palm tree features among Morocco's tree symbols. The palm grove of Marrakech was created by Yusuf ben Tashufin, who had 80,000 trees planted there at the end of the 11th century. The Umayyad sultans did the same at Elche and in all the strongholds of Al-Andalus in memory of Damascus and Baghdad, the "land of palms" that they had left in the 7th century.

The Jihel, Bou-Feggous and Mehjoul dates grown from the Tafilalet valleys to the Figuig oasis may not quite match the dates of Egypt, Iraq and Algeria, with its Deglet-Nour variety, but they are still blessings in the "favored Empire."

Morocco's cultivation of dates is not as widespread as it is among its neighbors—some 200,000 tons of dates earmarked for export as compared with Egypt's half a million—but it is still ever-present in the landscape and life of present-day Morocco, and in a particularly forceful way. Lively discussions about the ravages of the *Bayoud* (which has been rife since the late 19th century) and the "disease of the leaning heart" (which appeared in Mauritania in 1949), and the lot of the palm grove of Marrakech, fair game now for property developers, are never altogether formal. Perhaps they would be less impassioned, were the date palm not the symbol of the country's sound good health, sign of an ancestral favor shared with the other countries of Islam.

The mythical creation of the date palm has it born from Adam: "When God (may He be praised!) had created the world and driven Adam from Paradise, he made him descend to earth, then he ordered the archangel Gabriel, faithful guardian and messenger of celestial orders, to order Adam to wash himself completely, from head to toe, and handed him the scissors with which to cut his plentiful head of hair

With its cluster of palm fronds and its dates "like fingers of light," the palm tree is the country's Phoenix. As Africa's traditional feature since the 16th century, it proclaims from the top of its trunk both resurrection and life—the spring hidden beneath the sand and the glory of the air.

and trim his exceedingly long finger-nails—Adam complied with the orders of the Creator, whom he thanked with great praise, and, after washing himself, he buried his hair and nail clippings in the loam from which he himself had been created and formed in the image of God."[1] The palm tree is not just another tree; it is an uncle and a brother, a sort of benevolent plant double or "significant ally" which merits special consideration.

As the *Cairene Cheikh, Camel-Eddine,* suggests, the palm tree is doubly sacred, by virtue of its geography (which overlaps with the geography of Islam) and by virtue of its resemblance to the sons of Adam, "The palm tree is a blessed tree. It is only found in Muslim lands. The Prophet said: 'Be generous with your uncle the palm tree [...]. It is like man, in the uprightness of its size and its height, in its distinction between male and female, and the special nature of its fertilization. Were its head to be cut off, it would die; if its heart were exposed to some accident, it would perish.' "[2] So great care must be taken not to offend it and to follow its example. In his monumental *Kitab al-Filhala, The Book of Agriculture,* Ibn al-Awwan, the brilliant 12th-century agronomist from Seville, warned the farmer thus: "The man who plants a palm tree must have a lymphatic, lunar temperament, and his body must be in a normal state. He must be merry and smiling, with no pressures, and a figure with a look of well-being and good cheer."[3] Even though the Koran tells how King Seth, son of Adam, was the first to cultivate its fruit and if Alexander the Great got it to flourish throughout North Africa, and it served to shade Mary on her flight into Egypt, it is above all the Prophet's blessed tree, the tree that the archangel Gabriel caused to sprout forthwith from the earth with its "luxuriant foliage covered with succulent fruit," so that Muslims might eat their fill.

It is also the most useful of trees, as is clear from this *hadith* that can be read in Rissani and Erfoud during the date festival: "Be favorable to us, oh date palm, oh brother of Adam. You give us the date, in varieties we have lost count of. You give us your trunk to support our homes. Your palm fronds put together are a soft bed for us. Your fibres make ropes that are stronger than those made of camel hair. Your heart is like a pine that nurtures. Your blood is like a milk that refreshes in spring."[4]

The scenic tree. The palm tree is part of the orientalist's wherewithal. You'll see it blending with the distant mountain and the city walls, carefully set off-center and leaning, perfect prop for desert imagery, forlorn kouba and royal palace—he most obvious of exotic flourishes.

WATER

"FROM WATER WE HAVE MADE ALL LIVING THINGS"

A *seguia* making its way noiselessly on the hillside, the huge pool of an *aguedal* or royal orchard, the sparkling pond of a *riyad*, a fountain covered with *zelliges* in the middle of the *medina*, misted-up *hammams* where hot water spurts from the tap, "gurgling goatskin bottles"[1] straddling a camel's back—whatever its role, water in Morocco is a gift from God. The only other commodity so venerated is bread. In his Moroccan diary, Claude Ollier described how Moroccans "... make the most of water, of the merest trace of water. [Their] tremendous optimum utilization of dampness and wetness, the opposite of dryness, of incredible aridity, of all things shrivelled, sandy and dusty."[2] Water is the number one symbol. "From water We have made all living things, neighed and whinnied the horses echoing in response," to borrow the slightly odd words written by Driss Chraïbi, quoting the famous words of the Koran.[3]

Ever since the Middle Ages, Fez has boasted an ultra modern dual system of water distribution, but it couldn't have been created without its Vaucluse-like springs. Marrakech would not exist where it now stands, if the Almoravids hadn't been desert people accustomed to channeling water and taking it a long way from its source by way of underground qenat. Shella is a watering place.

All you have to do is walk into an Atlas village, or stop at a southern oasis, to realize to what extent mastery of water is the key to the Moroccan countryside. Back in the city, local fountains, veritable hubs of social life, give free rein to the coolness and the beauty of their ceramics like an embroidered shield. And how can one describe the delicacy with which people in Morocco actually touch water?

The survival of the hammam in the area around the mosque is a sure sign—though the traveller in search of a sensuous experience may forget it—that he is first and foremost partaking of a ritual of purification and cleansing that is half-social, half-religious. The "Moorish bath" was probably imported from Andalusia, where the Umayyads had encouraged its widespread use, modeled on the hammams of Damascus and Baghdad (which were themselves based on the example of the Byzantine steam room, the *hammamat rumiyya*, bequeathed by the Romans). It then developed apace in Morocco, to the point where in Fez alone, at the beginning of the 16th century (when Leo Africanus stayed there), there were more than a hundred such establishments in the city.

Its architecture, which is less impressive than in Istanbul, is always the same: the hammam always has a changing room, the *maslakh*; an in-between room, the *virdie barrani*, the "first apartment"; the less tepidly heated, so-called "middle" room; and the second heated room, the *harara*. As a place of purification, the hammam is also a meeting place where endless discussions take place; it is also one of those rare forums to which women have long had access and which, despite its current lapse of function resulting from tourism, is still a focal point of Moroccan social life.

Opposite: A hadith *puts it well: "the definition of paradise is prayer and the definition of prayer is toilet: O you who believe, when you prepare yourselves for prayer, wash your face, and your hands up to the elbows, clean your head and your feet up to the ankles."*
Following pages: *After creating the earth, the first child, the sun and the stars, writes Driss Chraïbi in* La mère du printemps, *the Nurturing Mother gave the water of the springs, of the* issafen *(rivers), seas and clouds, "...because above her, all around her, everything was dry."*

MILK

A SIGN OF WELCOME

Long before coffee, which appeared in the 16th century, and well before tea which didn't become Morocco's number one beverage until the mid-19th century, milk, ritually accompanied by dates, was the symbol of Moroccan hospitality and the welcome signal extended by the country's hosts. A Delacroix painting, produced in 1845, a few years after the painter's stay in Morocco and now in the Nantes Museum of Fine Art, titled: "L'Offrande du lait" (The Offering of Milk), shows a *Cherif* on horseback, dipping a finger into a large pitcher of milk being held out to him in a sign of submission. "Milk", writes Fatéma Hal, "isn't just something specially for children. For us, it's a beverage that's every bit as symbolic as water. Wherever you go, custom has it that the foreigner or stranger be welcomed with milk and dates. What would a marriage be if the betrothed pair hadn't exchanged milk and dates? Milk is purity, dates are sweetness."[1] At the entrance to the bridegroom's house, in the nuptial bedchamber, the young bride finds a copper platter with a bowl of milk, dates and the keys to the house. She won't touch the dates, whose dark hue is not a good omen, but she will ask the women of the household to share the milk and its beneficial whiteness with her.

Such alarm accompanies its absence that there is no utterance more desperate than: "I've lost the taste for milk." The general word used to describe it is *akh*. In his Tuareg/French dictionary, Charles de Foucauld points out that akh "...applies to the milk of women and animals, whatever its state: fresh and sweet, sour, curdled, going off, unpasteurized, boiled, condensed, etc."[2] Among the different sorts of milk drunk in Morocco, we find goat's and camel's milk, in addition to cow's milk. The first two are rarely drunk fresh, or without being mixed with cow's milk. Milk straight from the camel, light and frothy, is one of the most flavorful—depending on the plants grazed by the herd.

Moroccans may love soft cheeses of the "Vache qui rit" type, known, in its local version, more wittily as "Vache aimée" or "Vache bonheur" (Beloved Cow or Cow of Happiness), but, just like the other countries of Islam, they are great eaters of fermented cheeses, preferring hard, dry cheeses and dairy products. So yogurt is the dairy king. Ottoman in origin, yogurt was adopted in the 18th century and is always prominently displayed in medina shops. There can be no greater pleasure than drinking these *raïbi* on the spot. They are a sort of liquid yogurt tasting very like the yogurts that grandmothers used to concoct. Served sweetened or natural in thick glasses, they are sometimes mixed with bits of semolina cake, as in Meknes, not far from the old *mellah*. But the most delicious of all, and the rarest of these dairy products, is the *zeri'a*, made of crushed melon seeds mixed with full-fat milk and flavored with rose water and cinnamon.[3] This beverage, sipped in the *hammam*, is one of the refinements of women's Morocco, like the milk sprinkled with thyme that is traditionally drunk in the Berber villages of the High Atlas.

"Water is the soul," says a Berber proverb, "but milk makes us live."

BREAD

IN PRAISE OF BREAD

An everyday scene in a *medina*: a girl or a boy, a wooden tray covered with a white cloth balanced on the shoulder, carries bread to the *farran*, the usual neighborhood oven. The messenger walks along the lane, head held high, stopping for no one, as if the family compound were also moving with him. Nobody would dream of importuning the child, the fact is that bread is *haram*, something sacred, as is its bearer.[1] The child's destination may be as gloomy as a cave, cluttered with piles of wood, but it is still one of the neighborhood sanctuaries. Nothing sets it apart except the smell of hot bread wafting over the lane. The floor is often made of clay. Lofty shelves rise up in the half-light, filled with loaves. On feast days, there is feverish activity hereabouts, but usually the sooty hideaway offers no sign of life. Together with the fountain, the mosque and the *hammam*, the oven is one of the places by which you can recognize a neighborhood (and for which people are prepared to do battle). The oven-master, or *ferrah*, knows each and every house and home, and all the neighbors who entrust their bread to him; he knows what kind of bake is required, and he's acquainted with the family seal on each *khabbaz*, ensuring there'll be no mistake. The advent of the individual gas oven—those deluxe behemoths brandishing the "Affifi"[2] trademark—hasn't done away with the traditional oven, though its days may be numbered. Bread cooked to last for a whole month, which was still eaten in the 19th century in the north of the country, and which Auguste Mouliéras compared to a "soldier's biscuit," has long since been forgotten.[3] But the same goes for those bread substitutes made with bean flour, sweet acorns, pods, husks and green beans, which stood in for loaves of wheat and barley when drought ravaged the land. It's a long time since the disappearance of those bread-based "soups" which Arab travellers in the 12th century called *asallu*, like Al Idrisi among the Berber tribes. Gone is the hotpot of meat and wheat flavoured with cinnamon-scented fat, called *harisa*, into which they would crumble semolina bread, known as *fatit*. But something of all this still remains in couscous and in several other dishes where bread plays a part. Moroccan bread is a daily bread. It's eaten fresh, and often serves as a fork to mop up *tajines*. It comes in all shapes and sizes, loaves made of wheat and barley, wheaten bread, leavened bread, bread with herbs and seeds, plaited and braided loaves, decorated or not, loaves for festivals, *saghrir*, which are like breakfast blinis, and *rghaïf*, which are puff pastries or simple flat cakes with sesame seeds. Fatéma Hal notes that making bread is the primary act of the mistress of the house. The author of "Saveurs et gestes" adds: "Morocco is a civilization of bread" and the Moroccans a "...people of bread eaters."[4] Ulysses would have felt quite at home in this land.

Piles of round loaves in the souk. At home, they are laid in the tbak, a basket with a wicker or copper lid.
At meals bread is used as a utensil to "mop up" tajines and the sauces of couscous dishes or thicken the family harira.

TEA

THE CEREMONY OF HOSPITALITY

It is the master of the house (or, in his absence, his wife or a wordless *lalla* will assume the task) who patiently, religiously and with remarkable seriousness prepares tea before your very eyes. While every other dish and platter is lovingly cooked away from prying eyes, tea is keen to be seen. If you made tea in the kitchen, this would be disobeying the rules of hospitality.

Whatever else, the teapot must be proffered steaming hot, and the ceremony itself, which is always somewhat solemn, must end with "...the cascade of froth crowning the cadi's white turban, as they say, a sign of the tea's nobility and success."[1] The swinging of the teapot at dizzy heights, the liquid gushing melodiously forth, the gilded shaft of lightning through the air, the spreading aroma and the posture and elegance of the master of ceremonies—it is all part and parcel of the tea celebration. In it, the sequence of movements is just as important as the props and the quality of the ingredients. Noting how the two ritual trays make their stage entrance is already a sure sign—whether they are made of gilded metal or tinplate, chased or unadorned, covered, or not, with an embroidered serviette; and whether they are laid on the *seniya*, a sort of low metal furnishing, or the *tefor*, made of finely worked wood and painted, or on the actual floor of a *nouala*.

On the first tray there are three boxes: the largest contains crushed sugar, the second mint leaves, and the third, and smallest box, the tea itself. A special tumbler is there to rinse the teapot, hammer is used to break up the sugar lumps, and, in a complete service, there are several narrow-spouted scent *aspergilla* to imbue everything with orange blossom and rose water.

The second tray is earmarked for the metal teapot and the ranks of glasses. In the early 20th century, the silver teapots and trays in middle-class homes came from the Richard Wright works in Manchester, and the glasses were made of Saint-Louis crystal. Since then, the Turkish-style glass, decorated with little red and green patterns, has taken over everywhere. The person officiating washes his hands, asks Allah for protection, and starts by warming the teapot before taking the tea in one hand (in order to pass his *baraka* on to the tea), and then putting it at the bottom of the pot, to be covered with the mint leaves and crushed sugar. The tea is usually green tea from China, mixed with mint; the *Mentha viridis* of Meknes and Zerhoun, with its dark-colored, hard stems, is reputed to be more fragrant than the *roumia* of Fez. Then starts a whole series of decantings and stirring motions, moments of waiting, ears pricked for the right quiver, eyes meeting eyes and short invocations and discreet lapping, punctuated by additions of water, all designed to achieve the ideal harmony. In the south, custom has it that the first tea be the lightest and most bitter, the second strong and sweet, and the third syrupy and almost acrid.

One day, Paul Bowles was given tea oil. "That smells wonderful," he said to Ira Cohen, "you put a drop on a cigarette and the whole house smelt of freshly served hot tea. A very strong smell, delicious, like the aroma of mint tea."

The ceremony can go on for quite a while, as was described in 1790 by G. Lemprière, an English physician who went to Morocco to tend to the sultan's son: "The great courtesy being to offer tea to the person visiting one of his friends, nobody pays any heed to time: tea is always brought in; it is served on a very short-legged table. In Morocco it is made by mixing mint leaves and Tansy. When this mixture is well infused, it is poured into splendid Indian porcelain cups that are strikingly small. It is served without milk or cream, and a few cakes made of dried preserves. The small amount of this beverage that is served at once illustrates the whole importance that the Moors attach to it. A tea party lasts at least two hours; only rich people can drink it, because of its rarity in Barbary."[2] In Morocco it is accompanied by gazelle's horns, *msemen*, *makroute* and sweets from Rabat.

Tea didn't become a popular beverage until the mid-19th century, after the English—whose route to the Slavic countries had been barred following the Crimean War and the Baltic Sea blockade—in 1854, set up trading posts in Tangier and Mogador to sell their stock. Since then, tea has spread throughout Morocco and has become the favorite drink of city-dwellers and nomads, who prefer it to the infusions they drank previously. Tea also tends to oust milk and dates, those symbols of welcome, Moroccan-style. In every corner of the land tea is also the signal that a deal has been struck, (ah! the rug dealer's tea in anticipation, when the customer is already lost!), that a transaction has been finalized, or that you have just had a good meal. But it is above all the symbol of sociability and togetherness, the proof of exchange—no matter how tenuous—as Roland Barthes notes in "Incidents," "On the road from Marrakech to Beni-Mellal, a poor adolescent, Abdelkhaïm, who speaks no French, is carrying a rough round basket. I give him a lift for a few hundred yards. No sooner than he is in the car, and he produces from his basket a teapot and hands me a glass of hot tea (but how can it be hot?); then he gets out, and vanishes at the side of the road."[3] The miracle of Moroccan tea.

As a symbol of togetherness, welcome and communion, observes E.A. El-Maleh, tea has given rise to
"...a ceremony steeped in know-how, discreet pleasure, solemnity and meditative patience."

TAJINE

BENEATH THE POINTED HAT, THE ART OF SWEET-AND-SAVORY

Together with couscous, *harira* and *bastella*, *tajine* is the best-known dish in the Moroccan cuisine. The word refers equally to the food itself and the glazed earthenware dish, the tajine *slaoui*, that has become the speciality of Sala. The dish consists of a hollow platter, in which is served the endless variety of preparations issuing from the lively imagination of Morocco's dada, and the crucial part of the edifice, the lid, shaped like a pointed hat.

The success of the tajine, writes Fatéma Hal, is such that it has ended up by "eclipsing almost all our other ways of cooking, as far as the public at large is concerned. To the point where, in Morocco itself, the word 'tajine' has become a generic word for describing the dish, any old dish—especially, I would even venture to say, if it's not cooked in a tajine."[1] The tajine is actually often cooked in the *taoua*, the round casserole dish made either of tinplated copper or cast iron (or in the simple *qadra*, the family casserole). The tajine slaoui (may it be blessed!) is used for keeping the various sorts of meat and their garnish hot on the *kanoun*, until it is time to sit down and eat.

The most classic tajine is a dish of braised chicken or lamb—more rarely beef—with onions, almonds, lemons and prunes, and a lengthy list of spices, headed by saffron, coriander and cumin, and served with a well-thickened sauce. Among the 101 more sophisticated recipes, which all call for meat cut into chunks and cooked until golden brown with diced onions, vegetables and quartered fruit that are simmered over a gentle flame before adding broad beans, carrot preserves and artichoke hearts, and every manner of herb, we should make mention of the marrakchi tajines, with tomatoes, broad beans and cinnamon-spiced wild artichokes; certain High Atlas tajines with peppers and eggs, and the pumpkin-based Mderbel tajine; a tajine made with quinces and unpeeled pears cut into two, with preserved pomegranate seeds and apricots, so similar to Andalusian cooking; Lham Mhammar tajine colored with hot red pepper and spiced with garlic and ginger; the sheep's-liver tajine with hot red pepper, and Qamama tajine, laced with saffron and crispy.

Nor should we overlook the family tajine commonly described as being "salvaged," i.e., made from leftovers, with stale bread, broad beans, tomatoes and onions gleaned from the depths of the kitchen, and, to wind up this brief listing, the royal Tanjia with lamb, spices and lemon preserves, cooked for a whole night in the embers of the *farnatchi*, the *hammam* furnace.

The tajine is the vessel of flavors—the architectural shape closest to perfect bliss.
It is to Moroccan cooking what the riyad is to architecture: a promise of happiness.

HENNA

THE FLESH-COLORED BALM OF PROTECTION

As the Arab geographer Al Idrisi made his way across the western Sous, he was struck by the flaming fair hair of the inhabitants, and duly observed: "They let their hair grow and tend to it with much care indeed, dyeing it each week with henna, and washing it twice a week with egg white and whiting."[1] Henna—the "plant of paradise"—may not be quite so ubiquitous these days, but it is still the principal ingredient in the beauty products and magic rituals of traditional Morocco. Nor is its use by any means peculiar to this country, for it is used in countless ways from the Atlantic to the Ganges. Henna lies at the heart of the home and the *hammam*, the very symbol of protection.

Archaeologists have found traces of it dating back to 1235 BCE in the hair of Ramses II, in the tombs of the kings of Mycenae, among the Persians and Assyrians, in Babylon and in Persepolis. Mahomet used it to dye his beard and hair.

In Morocco, henna is grown in the Tafilalet, the Sous and around Azemmour. Its scientific, Linnaean name is *Lawsonia inermis*. Its ivory-white flower gives off a heady scent of mignonette. But it's the henna leaves that you find in bulk in great baskets in the *souks* of Fez and Marrakech. And the henna base is green paste made from these great piles of leaves. To produce this mud with its slightly coarse texture, you must grind up the leaves with a pestle and dampen them with rose water perfumed with myrtle and orange blossom.

Henna has spectacular dyeing properties. Fatima Mernissi describes in detail the four varieties, without which the henna experts, gathered for the occasion in the courtyard of the house, would not get what they want: "For those who want red highlights, henna was diluted with a boiling juice of pomegranate bark and a pinch of carmine. For those wanting darker hues, the henna was mixed with a lukewarm juice of walnut stain. And for those who simply wanted to strengthen their hair, henna mixed with tobacco could work wonders. For women looking for a moisturizing treatment, the henna took on a more watered down texture, mixed with olive oil, argan nuts and almonds, before being massaged into the scalp."[2]

Henna is not applied solely to the hair, it is used on hands and feet, too, either in the form of a uniform patch or drawn on with the help of a *stylet*. To make these fine patterns with their geometric motifs, Morocco relies on the know-how of the *hennayat*, those henna specialists with their notebooks filled with designs, who offer their services in souks. But henna is also used for dyeing the tufts, manes and tails of horses being prepared for the *fantasia* or equestrian performance; it is also a tool for marking sheep—those sheep whose eyes are made up with kohl—on the eve of the Aïd el-Kebir.

Henna and the magical properties that go with its applications are inseparable, and it plays a major part in rites of passage. "Covering your feet with henna," wrote the Tharaud brothers, "even in the ordinary

The scent of its flower is somewhere between jasmine, tea rose and mignonette. Its natural color tends toward tawny red.
Its medicinal properties are anti-bacterial and coagulant. Its magic powers are countless. On the hands, feet and face henna wards off the evil eye.

course of life, is always a celebration, an opportunity to invite friends and hire the *chirat* or female singer. People like the baked-bread color left by this coating on the skin, and the gem- or ruby-like aspect it lends the fingernails; and above all, as there is an ever-present risk of brushing against air and water spirits, it is both wise and courteous that they only be touched with feet and hands which are also pleasant to look at and smell."[3] On the eve of her wedding day, the bride-to-be spends the *leilat al-hanna* or henna night, with the women of the two families involved; on this night, the "great henna ceremony" is carried out, usually in the hammam reserved for the occasion--on the head, hands (where the eye that will drive evil spirits away is drawn) and feet, not forgetting the casting of the seven balls of henna to the jnoun through the drain, while uttering the ritual sentence: "O lords of the earth, this is your share". After rinsing the henna with the help of the ghassoul—a particularly Moroccan shampoo of dried brown clay scented with rose and myrtle water which is prepared in the home—the hennayat sings: "I comb you with happiness/ I comb you with the plant of happiness/ You will be mistress of the house."[4] The day after the wedding night, purifying, cleansing henna is for bride and groom alike. A year later, the hennayat re-enacts the great henna ceremony and draws the magic square in the palm of the bride's right hand, a pledge of the stability of the marriage. When the first child is born, henna is used to heal the scar on the navel. When the infant is first washed, a little powder from the magic plant will be scattered to ward off evil spirits; seven days after the baby's birth, it is time to put some henna on the mother's right ankle, so she will get off on the right foot, as well as on her hands, so that she will pass on the henna's luck and blessings to her child. Forty days later, new henna will be applied to wind up the birth cycle. Henna is also used when someone dies, to guide the deceased towards paradise. A girl who passes away before being engaged will receive henna so as to make her marriage easier in the hereafter. On the eve of a battle, the soldier will have henna put on his right hand. There is also a pilgrimage henna which is pressed with splayed hands onto the whitewashed wall of the *kouba*, as there is a jealousy henna, a thieves' henna, a henna for departure and homecoming, a henna marking the end of mourning and a henna marking the beginning of fasting.

Henna is a mystery. It alerts the eye for curses and protects against humiliation by weaving a fine web of lines, but it is also an instrument of seduction; it lends the skin and hair the colour of a smoldering fire--it is the embers of passions and desires.

THE HAÏK

FABRIC UPON FABRIC

The first traveller to pay it any close heed was Pidou de Saint-Olon, Louis XIV's ambassador at the court of Mawlay Ismail. His description of men's clothing gives us a more or less comprehensive picture of the 17th century Moroccan gentleman's wardrobe—a quite short shirt with long sleeves rolled back over the shoulders, the present-day *tchamir* or *qmis*, and "linen underpants not extending below the knee"; babouche slippers; a caftan: "a sleeveless woollen jacket of any color the wearer might desire"; a *haïk*: "...which is a length of very fine white woollen fabric, about five *ells* in length and one and a half in width, used to cover the head and body around which it is wrapped several times, under and over the arm, in the same way that one sees in the drapery of ancient figures," and a *burnous*, which is known as the *selahm* in Morocco: "...a sort of coat or cloak made of wool or woollen cloth trimmed with a fringe, with a hood hanging down behind, and a tassel at the tip."[1] In 1832, Delacroix noticed the brief and dazzling appearances of a dark blue burnous, a red haïk, a yellow cafetan, a dark blue haïk and cafetan, and a purple belt embroidered with gold, among a thousand "different little things everywhere," which he painted in watercolors in his sketchbooks like so many petals of pure color, so he could later refer to them in his Parisian canvases. The greenish-blue costumes of Zorah and the flamboyant clothes of the man from the Rif would all similarly be pure flourishes of color for Matisse, in 1912-1913, during his sojourn in Tangier. Two years later, Gatian de Clerambault, a Parisian psychiatrist at the Special Infirmary of the Paris Police Headquarters, during a trip to Morocco photographed groups of women in their haïks. He thus embarked on a long series studying "Mediterranean drape" and those strange "fabric enthusiasts" who the police would bring to him because they were unable to resist the "call of silk" in the departments brimming with taffeta, tarlatan, mull and other types of muslin at Bon Marché.[2] The way colonial people viewed Moroccan clothing would be very different. Gone were Loti's short-lived enchantments, (he who had a tendency to take the color out of everything and cover Moroccan people and things with a white shroud). The Tharaud brothers saw nothing but uniformity in the street: men and women, they wrote "... are dressed more or less the same way. They both wear the same broad-sleeved cotton shirt, whose embroidered collar, clinging to the neck, is attached to the shoulder by a thin cord; the same buttoned caftan... and the same *farajiyya*, the same muslin surplice, so it is quite common for a husband to borrow his wife's caftan, and a wife her husband's. To the unaccustomed eye, all these clothes, cut on the same stencil, seem to have nothing whatsoever to do with personal whim."[3] In the period 1934-1938, Jean Besancenot would soon embark on a listing of the huge range of clothes in Morocco, just as Prosper Ricard had done for carpets and rugs.[4] But the venture fizzled out. In complete contrast with the viewpoint of the Tharaud brothers, the present-day situation with Moroccan clothing is governed by variety and a great deal of fantasy.

The way the haïk is tied in Fez is not the way the women of Marrakech do it, and the way they do it in the deep south differs from the way they do it in Tetouan. The blue izar of Goulimine has neither the colors, nor the dimensions, nor the pleats of the large piece of rough cloth worn by the men of the Rif. The haïk enjoys a varied geography.

What you see in the street, mixing the standards of traditional clothing and the clothes of western soci-eties, is one of the most sensational sights in the Maghreb. Walking down an Essaouira street, past a woman clad in the southern *tamelhat*, the black cloth hemmed with red thread on the shoulders, wearing on her head a black band decorated with little mock-coral-like plastic sticks; her head covered with a red haïk, and a young woman reading a European fashion magazine, in a sexy suit and high heels; such are the contrasting symbols of ways of dressing that people would like to hold on to. But the real situation is more complicated; plenty of examples of tradition intermingling with innovation are at work in today's Morocco, which numbers many *Zyriab*[5] ready to renew the hallowed models of classic clothing. One of the areas where creative endeavor is at its freest is jewelry and makeup, with all their countless symbolic and magical meanings. These days, Casablanca and Rabat are the twin cities of Moroccan fashion—at the intersection where design meets the visual arts.

Opposite: *The same goes for caftans: the large, long, collarless and hoodless garment, with its wide sleeves, which is worn open at the front, comes in many different forms: velvet or silk, with gold and silver thread, brocaded, damasked, decorated with arabesques, or severe and unadorned.*
Following pages: *Finery. If, as Khaïr Eddine laments, "…modernization is gradually nibbling away at the age-old beauty of things," and replacing the coral rods of southern head-dresses with plastic sticks and silver buckles, and heavy amber necklaces with safety pins and thin cords, Moroccan finery still has a sheer and sumptuous quality to it.*

BABOUCHES

THE BAREFOOT SHOE

The *babouche* hails from the East and means in Persian "covered foot." Its use spread to Morocco by way of the Andalusians from the 9th century on. The babouche is the typical footwear of city-dwelling Islam. "It is designed in such a way," writes L. Brunot, "that you can easily remove it, at any given moment, when you go into a bedroom, say, and put it back on to cross a courtyard or street... in town it is more often at the door to a room, shop, or place of prayer than on its owner's feet."[1] Travelling painters depict it sometimes on the sultan's foot, like Delacroix, drawing the "...yellow slippers which are open at the back" as worn by Mawlay Abd er-Rahman; sometimes, as in "Les femmes d'Alger," on the foot of a slave or else set beside the young Zorah, like Matisse in Tangier. In the bazaar, the variety of models of babouche intrigued Théophile Gautier, who was amazed by "those shelves filled with extravagant shoes, with the toes turned up like Chinese roofs, with flattened flaps, made of leather, morocco, velvet, brocade, quilted, sequined, spangled, trimmed with braid, embellished with tassels of down and silk, impossible for European feet."[2] The babouches of Morocco are no less varied: "...there is no courtier," wrote Leo Africanus of the babouches of Fez, "soldier or craftsman who dares wear babouches of the same type and beauty."[3] They invariably consist of a backless leather sole, a large upper whose opening fits as tightly as possible, and a flap folded over the heel. Men's babouches are yellow or cream-colored for ceremonies, unadorned apart from the *sarma*, the silk thread that runs parallel with the stitching along the edge of the upper, or embroidered with arabesques. The least refined sort, the *mesarbla*, which is preferred by craftsmen and workers for its sturdiness and blunt shape, differs from the babouche of *makhezni* and wealthy merchants, lined with cloth, known as *madfuna* or *msahbra*, the "shopping shoe."

Women's babouches come in two types, each one with an infinite variety of models; the *massaya* designed for indoor use, and the *ribiya* for outings. They are yellow, black and red, decorated with silk embroidery in every color. By way of their variety, babouches offer a good way of getting an idea of Moroccan society: Driss Chraïbi imagines a camera, positioned just above ground level, filming "...a pair of bare feet with rough heels in tan babouches: their owner is probably a grocer or a donkey-driver; stockings of thick, colored wool and babouches with thick rubber soles: perhaps a *fiqh*, to which people give a little *fabor*... perhaps, too, a *muezzin*, a *Dellaline* broker, or a tobacco merchant; male legs sheathed in white silk and feet delicately fitted into fine pale yellow or white babouches, so-called 'doctor's' babouches, betraying a notary, a businessman, an imam, an artist or an idle rich man; but there are also shoes, sandals, naïls, and bare feet, these latter bearing oven boys and school dunces."[4]

"A family of chorfas owned a pair of babouches that was said to have belonged to the Prophet Muhammad. Mawlay Ismaïl was forever trying to acquire them. Once he took possession of them, he erected a cupola'd temple inside his palace at Meknes."

THE FANTASIA

IN PRAISE OF DUST

The *fantasia* is a fantasy, an equestrian performance put on as a sign of welcome, or for a *moussem*. At once a show of strength and warrior prowess, designed to impress those watching, it is also a sport and an entertainment, one of the rare such manifestations to have been encouraged by the Prophet, and symbol of the traditions of romantic "old Morocco." The word fantasia, of Spanish origin, describes, first and foremost, something that is proud-looking and carried out with panache. In 1847, Delacroix used it for the first time in the title of a painting: "Una fantasia au Maroc" (A Fantasia in Morocco), which he painted shortly after his journey there, from a watercolor[1] in memory of a fantasia outside Meknes. Raging gallop captured in midair, billowing white robes, rifles whirling against the sky, wild faces, clouds of dust and golden sand: the painting would establish a new genre, from Chasseriau to Fromentin.

In the *darija* tongue, the fantasia is called *tburida*, which means "in praise of dust"; for the Berbers, it means parade or prancing, a dazzling *volte* or spin. The fantasia actually combines the *la'b al-baroud*, the "dust game" and the *çibaq al-khayl*, the "equestrian game."

The way the race works is simple enough. On a cleared piece of ground, a safe distance from the caïd's tents, where the guests of honor and the race's judges are seated, a line of riders gets ready for the off, twenty mounts or more. In 1969, the "Fantasia of the Century" held in Rabat for the king's 40th birthday—the king being a great lover of horses and equestrian traditions, which he helped to revive—brought 2000 competitors together for the occasion.

To the cry of "In the name of God and to the glory of the Prophet!" the start is sounded; the riders make a first *baroud*, a circuit run at a fast trot, enabling them to introduce themselves, then all return together to the starting line. The race proper can now begin: a short, restrained trot which, after some fifty yards, turns into a gallop which grows faster and faster over the next 150-200 yards. The riders are standing upright in their stirrups. In unison they all start "making the dust talk," as Pierre Loti wrote, "slackening all their reins on their bolting steeds, waving their long rifles in the air, at the end of their bare arms jutting from *burnouses* swept along by the wind."[2] Loti doesn't mention any pauses, just the unbroken series of charges. The fantasia, these days, ends up with the horses all pulled up short just a few feet from the tent of honor.[3] Meanwhile, the wild and frenzied show has imposed some rules on itself. The fantasia will be graded on the precise alignment of the charge, the straightness of its run, its speed, the synchrony of the rifle fire, the cohesion, appearance and elegance of the horsemen and their mounts. Just like an Olympic discipline.

Opposite: *The troop of horsemen "… bristling with long thin rifles;*
swathed in white," which fascinated Pierre Loti.
Following pages: *"When an order is barked by the chiefs, they come back flat out,*
in small groups, at a wild gallop, right towards us—Brr! Brr!" (P. Loti, Au Maroc).

JNOUN

GOOD AND EVIL SPIRITS

Morocco is the chosen land of the *jnoun*, those spirits of the invisible world who camp on the edge of the desert, close to the lights of the night and the "sea of darkness." They are called "those from below." They are strangers on earth, odd companions with ephemeral identities and forms, roaming in the twilight. They are known as "the sons of solitude" and "the sons of the deep earth."

The etymology of jinn probably doesn't come from Latin genius, or genie, but rather from the Arabic root janna, which means "to cover," "wrap," and "that which is concealed from the gaze." For example, the embryo, the foetus, the heart, everything that is hidden deep-down, like the earth before Allah created the world.

Generally speaking, the *jinn* involves everything that defies understanding. It may be visible or invisible, man or woman, airborne or terrestrial, kind or cruel, and it may like or shun noise. Its ability to move very fast, to propagate or stay stock-still, and its fondness for unexpected changes and disguises are fearsome. It gives us an idea of what the world might be like if God had not sorted it out by revealing its uniqueness to the Prophet.

When the spirit ventures into a human body, its presence may go unnoticed, or it may unexpectedly come to the fore. In other cases, the jinn will opt for a powerful method, manifesting itself as epilepsy, catatonia, or any other phenomenon of being possessed, as in the *lila*, the nights of the *Gnaoua*.

Its favorite creatures are the black cat, the frog, the wild boar, the tortoise, the young bull, the *fennec*, the ant, and all animals that live by night and inhabit dark crannies. But for the same reasons it may also wake up as a snake, scorpion, hedgehog, jerboa or mouse.

Its preferred places are just as varied: it may be a tree or a box room, a drain or a barren moor, the threshold of a home or a dank cave, the muggy *hammam* or burning sand, the ridge beam of a house or a pitcher at the back of a kitchen cupboard.

Confronted with this kind of versatility, all manner of stratagem is called for: the incantotions, gestures and amulets to protect us from jnoun are legion. Among the commonest, there is allegedly nothing more effective than salt or the fumes of incense and benzoin, the jinn having been created, so the Koran tells us, from a smokeless flame. But one of the most tried and tested methods is still to give the spirit its due, at the end of the harvest or during a wedding feast.

Be they she-devils turned into whirls of purple cinders, wandering shadows or unbridled ghouls, the jnoun also walk the backstreets of the medina in smart clothes; their path may cross yours at any moment—a sign or two will be enough for you to dodge them.

ZELLIGE

BRIGHT AND COLORFUL GEOMETRY

The art of the *zellige*—*zillig* in Arabic—originated in Morocco in the Roman mosaics of Volubilis, Lixus and Benara. Like mosaic, the zellige is a multi-colored decoration, made by inlaying a mass of small pieces embedded and set with cement, to a wall or floor. But unlike the regular cubes of the mosaic (the *teserae*), the zellige requires pieces cut out in different geometric shapes (rectangles, squares, lozenges, bezants, leaves, etc.), the *frem* which dovetail together to form radial patterns and motifs (star-shaped polygons, *khamsa*, stars of David, rosettes etc.) and simple alignments with endlessly varying combinations. The small pieces are cut from terra cotta tiles, measuring four by four inches, dried in the sun, flattened, smoothed and chamfered for the first firing, then enameled and fired again, before being re-cut and delivered to 'zelligers' or zillig-makers in large baskets in which the cutter has arranged them by category. Already in evidence in Central Asia, Iran and Turkey, the zellige made its appearance in Morocco in the late 12th century on the outer friezes of the *koutoubia* and the mosque in the Marrakech *casbah*, as in the *medersa*, the *zaouïa* and the mosques of the imperial cities on both shores of the Mediterranean. In the early 16th century, Leo Africanus observed, as he strolled through Fez, many porticos of houses whose columns were "...half covered with majolica," colleges with "walls embellished by mosaics with carved architraves," like the Seffarine built between 1321 and 1323, arches, "all enhanced by majolica"; "beautiful, low fountains made with majolica," and the tanks of Abu Inan, "covered with admirable work."[1] In Morocco, the zellige often covers walls at about the height of a person, as well as the entire floor. It clads patios with its dazzling texture, as for some never-ending reception. Its use, and its "drape-like" styles, are the architectural transcription of nomadic welcome rituals, which honor the guest by setting on the floor and walls—in some cases by overlaying them—the family clan's precious fabrics and loveliest rugs. The rite of covering up the *Ka'ba* with the *kiswa*, that heavy, formerly multicolored, embroidered fabric, conjures up the same ceremonial welcome. Like the carpet from which it borrows its panel-like composition and its arrangement on the floor, the zellige is a geometric art. The eye glances over its rosettes, its alignments of stars and lozenges, without dwelling on any one motif in particular. In Islam, writes Oleg Grabar"... geometry is a perfect go-between, for it attracts attention not to itself but to places and functions other than itself."[2]

Opposite: *Star-shaped polygons, rectangles on their tips, rosettes, brocaded friezes, rows of bezants, epigraphic decorations, fans, trails of leaves, Vedic squares, circles, spirals, pentagons—the ways of the zellige are countless.*
Following pages: *The zellige completely covers the surface it decorates. It is a carpet and a ceramic drape. For its textile-like effect to be at its fullest, it must create an impression of general swathing, where the light juggles with highlights and reflections, bursts of color, and dazzling air.*

RUGS AND CARPETS

FAMILY HERITAGE AND EVERYDAY INVENTION

They are less famous than the kilim of Anatolia and, at first glance, less refined than Persian carpets. Their reputation is that of tribal weavings with primitive accents, which European taste discovered in the 1920s, after the colonial inventory drawn up by Prosper Ricard,[1] for their geometric rusticity and the straightforwardness and freedom of their colorful improvisation. Is this *Chiadma* of Essaouira really too irregular, wine lees with lopsided stitching with its interrupted patterns, its switches of mood, and its brilliant tangents? Is this *Rabat*, or this *Mediouna* from near Casa too bright, naively mimicking its oriental model with its fleshy motifs? Are these *Beni Ouaraïn* of the Middle Atlas too severe, tight woven and short-piled as they are, on their fine network of small black lattice-work on a white ground? The rugs and carpets of Morocco have the unpredictable texture of a living language. It is impossible not to stand awe-struck before the *Beni Sadden* of the Middle Atlas with their wide-eyed figures, red and gold; or the gold-tinged finery of an *Aït Youssi*, the purple splendor of the carpets of Zemmour, the unbelievable architecture of a *Glaoua* of the High Atlas, all black and white, the delicacy of a *Chichaoua* of the Haouz (the lowlands) of Marrakech, golden pollen on red sand, or the changing bedazzlement of an *Oulad Bousbaa....*

Moroccan rugs and carpets are actually a kaleidoscope of expertise and know-how, inventiveness, and local traditions which the aesthetic viewpoint cannot comprehend on its own, unaided. The carpet is not merely a beautiful object for the eye; it is the home's garden of paradise, the symbol of the hearth of hospitality and the logbook of the lives of the women who make them. In the al-Ghashiyah sura--meaning "that which covers"—the Koran describes it as the reward of the righteous: "Because of their hard work on earth, satisfied, in a lovely garden where they will hear no prattle, where there is a gushing spring, where there are raised beds, craters set down, cushions neatly arrayed, and carpets laid flat."

The host honors his guest by laying out his finest carpets, pride of the family circle, a possession so precious that people will agree to lend them for grand occasions, but will definitely never sell them, unless literally forced to do so. The carpet is a living heritage, it is the living memory of the family and the symbol of its continuity and permanence. Its making is shrouded in rituals designed to attract good spirits to it, for a carpet that might bring the evil eye would be disastrous for the household. Weaving is no ordinary activity, and there are days when the loom is best left at rest. Each stage will come with set formulas--hanging amulets, the exclusion of boys, etc., "The most mute and most discreet of carpets," notes A. Khatibi, "holds a secret store, not just of symbols... but of the nerves of the imagination...."[2]

Opposite: *Le Corbusier was fond of Zaïne and Aït Ouaraïn carpets, and invited European artists*
"to do like the Berbers: combine geometry with wild fantasy." Kandinsky owned several carpets.
Klee and Matisse drew inspiration from them, on account of this freedom, avoiding the "dictates of wool."
Following pages: The loom. The usual width of a rural carpet is five feet. When the timber is stouter
and the room accommodating the loom much larger, the carpet may be proportionately wider still,
but in such cases two women will have to work on it.

HLAYKI

STORYTELLERS AND CHARLATANS

They are called *hlayki*, which means, literally: "those who make a circle." You'll find them on the Jemaa el-Fna square in Marrakech, and on the Derb Ghallaf in Casablanca, on the outskirts of country souks, on a piece of waste ground in city suburbs, and by a gate or door. Invariably standing there, gesticulating fiercely, forefinger placed at the eye, pulling the skin downward, the eye upturned and skyward, exclaiming: chouf! chouf! Look! Look!—hand on a megaphone, or else sitting cross-legged, murmuring tales. They are pedlars and smooth talkers, gembri players, snake-charmers, monkey trainers and scorpion tamers, tarantula tamers, too, jacks-of-all-trades, in exchange for a few unashamedly inveigled *dirhams*. They look down their noses at tourists unable to understand them, and talk solely to the Moroccan audience. Elias Canetti saw them at work on Jemaa el-Fna: "It's the storytellers who draw the largest crowds. Around them the most numerous and loyal listeners form circles. Their tales are a long time in the telling. Those listening crouch down forming the first circle on the ground, and are never in a hurry to stand back up again. Others, standing, form a second circle. They hardly move at all, spellbound, hanging on the storyteller's words and gestures."[1] There's the classic storyteller, fewer and fewer these days; there's the "trendy sex" merchant, by far the most popular, with his little cardboard store of potions for curing venereal diseases, who delights the audience with strictly forbidden expressions; the preacher of apocalyptic events; the herbalist in the midst of his little stand filled with magic substances, phials and animal carcasses, offering an ointment that puts everything to right "from head to toe;" the marriage counselor; the clairvoyant, a bit on the sidelines; the astrologer, the futuristic trickster with his miraculous computer, which delves into souls and bodies in a flash. They all live off of handouts, half beggar, half pedlar, subscribing to those "illegal little trades" on the outer edges of the economy, who, along with all the street kids, make up the day-to-day life of the Moroccan city. Their survival, despite radio and TV, can be explained by this very life on the fringe, and by the liberties taken here, come what may, with official censorship and discourse. For in these "charlatan's words," social caricature, the farce of politics and all the burning frenzy of a language that has been stifled come through.

In Jemaa el Fna square, writes Juan Goytisolo, "… the storyteller with his suggestive, biting, explosive eloquence, which makes clever use of the skills of popular speech—unhampered jargon, uncensored and uninhibited—tales of love and cuckoldry and intrigue, all interwoven."

KHAMSA

THE HAND OF FATIMA

It is quite surprising to find it in any number of forms, in a country where figurative symbols are not common currency. Where do they come from, these hands you see here, there and everywhere, with their splayed fingers, and their thumbs cocked either up or downward—for they crop up on car windscreens, and in house doorways, printed with henna on the outer walls of sanctuaries, or roughly painted with lime on the façade of a house being built; tulip-shaped or in the form of a mihrab; cut out in plaques nielloed with gold and silver, decorated with stars, animals and flowers, used as a pendant; fashioned from sugar and dough; embroidered and woven into the pile of carpets and drawn in sand: where do they all come from? Is it the white hand of Moses? The open hand, be it Chaldean or Punic, the Roman fica? The hands of Jupiter? Tanit? Baal? The hand of the five commandments of Mahomet?

The symbol of the hand is a migrating animal. In Morocco it is adopted by Berbers, Arabs and Jews alike as a talisman against evil spells. Islam attributes it to Fatima, the thumb symbolizing *Mahomet* and the fingers the four "perfect woman: Fatima, daughter of the Prophet, Khadijah, his wife (Fatima's mother), the Virgin Mary and Asiya, wife of the Pharaoh, who Moses saved from the Nile, and made him her adopted son. Its preventive effectiveness is formidable: "It works," wrote J. Herber, "like a spike, like the stake of Ulysses."[1] When somebody looks to be on the verge of giving you the evil eye, there is no better way to parry it than the khamsa; you just hold out the hand, palm outwards and fingers set apart, and say in clear tones: *khamsa fi 'aïnik*—"five (fingers) in your eye"—to send the evil packing right back to the person it came from. If the threat persists and becomes greater, you will say *Zob fi 'aïnik*, trying not to utter the words too loud, so as not to offend the spirits. As a general rule, and for the same reasons, you should avoid referring to the figure five, getting round this thorny problem with expressions like "the total of your hand," "three plus two" or "four plus one." For five brings good luck. In the Muslim week, Thursday, *al khamis*, the day of circumcision, the day people get married, or when you go on a pilgrimage or to market; in short, the day when you embark on things though you're not sure how they'll turn out, but hope they'll turn out well. To be even more sure, it is not advisable to wear the khamsa next to your skin, decorated with an eye, a star or Solomon's seal.[2]

The white hand of Moses, with a crocodile snaking across it here, certainly drives away evil spirits by its sheer power--the hand itself, symbol of authority, the legendary power of the creature that is king of the Nile with its fearsome jaws. Watch out, if you rub against it!

THE MOUSSEM

THE TIME OF THE NOUBAS

Between June and October, Morocco lives to the rhythm of the *moussem*, those country festivals which galvanize certain imperial cities like Fez, Sala and Meknes. Based on the model of the age-old seasonal festivals of pre-Islamic antiquity, these cyclical meetings coincide with harvest time, and come to a head in September. The moussem are associated with the worship of local saints, and are an occasion for pilgrimages and magic rituals accompanied with dancing and musical *noubas*. As a meeting-point for communities scattered over wide areas, they are also farming fairs with a fairly significant economic role to play. Families flock to them to sell the product of the latest harvests, haggle over the sale of livestock and handiwork made in the *douar*, purchase machine-tools, meet people and, in general, have fun. Some moussem, like the one at Imilchil, are famous for engagements and marriages, which are signed and sealed in the presence of the *adoul*, amid a great hubbub and display of costumes, make-up, music and dance. Others are famed above all for their *fantasias*, as at Mawlay Abdellah.

Many more recently concocted festivals celebrate a local culture, like the rose festival in the Dadès or the M'Goun, the date festival at Erfoud, the cherry festival at Sefrou and the almond festival at Tafraout.[1]

One of the most important moussem in Morocco, the moussem of Mawlay Abdellah Amghar, a mile or two from El Jedida, brings together each year a throng of more than 50,000 people, who camp out beside the ocean for a whole week in a makeshift canvas city. Everyone visits the tomb of Mawlay Abdellah Amghar, but the days are nevertheless quickly given over to merry-making and festive trading. The vast picnic offers visitors a chance to spend a week living at the pace of city life, with temporary cafés and restaurants everywhere, fair games and endless *souks*, strolls by night, chatting up those who catch your eye, and every manner of intrigue, bringing together city-dwellers hailing from Casablanca and Rabat and country-folk from southern Morocco. Likewise, the pilgrimage at Goulimine to the sanctuary of Sidi Ahmed Aanaro is an excuse for taking part, for three-days, in one of the major camel markets in all North Africa. Behind the folkloric—and very touristic—marriages at Imilchil between Aït Haddida, Aït Yazza and Aït Brahim, large-scale financial transactions, on which depend the following year's profits for the entire region, are being played out.

The moussem which have retained their religious character are organized by confraternities. The white-clad Aïssaouas have been gathering since the 17th century around the tomb of Mohamed ben Aïssa al-Mukhtari in Meknes. Several days of ceremonies, where music, dancing, mystical trances and sacrifices all play a crucial part.

The Hamadchas, faithful to Sidi Ali ben Hamdouch, a 17th century saint, gather around the tomb of

The moussem is a huge seasonal popular festival, often the occasion for a confraternity or guild to bring its patriarchs together; dressed in their finest jellabas, they are at the festival on patio benches—pensive sentinels of Morocco's traditions.

their master and his disciple Sidi Ahmed Dghoughi in the Zerhoun, east of Meknes, and make pilgrimages to Essaouira and Taroudant.

Every year, the Regragas leave the village of Akemoud in the south, site of their zaouïa, to visit the 44 sanctuaries of the Chiadma tribe.

The Gnaousa, hailing from the Bambara, Foula and Haoussa tribes, claim ancestry from the Ethiopian Bilal, the Prophet's first companion and *muezzin*. Their rallying point, for want of any *kouba*, is Essaouira, where, for several nights in a row, they carry out the ritual of the *lila* in the *Souiri* dwellings to which they are invited. But you will come across them in other Moroccan cities, such as Marrakech on the Jemaa el-Fna, and under roofs other than those of the Souiri faithful. After sacrificing the lamb and covering the distance between the Abdelkader *zaouïa* and the heart of Essaouira, the Gnaoua musicians embark upon their night's work. This lasts from nightfall to daybreak, and consists of three principal acts. The first is a kind of joyous preparation, a sort of warm-up, where the sound of the *bendir*, the *gembri* and the *ghayta* all mingle together, with singing, ritual invocations, and plenty of kif and tea.

The second, called the *meksa*, is a ritual summons to the spirits; metal rattles and explosive *qerqebat* come into play, with *kouyou* dances, designed to make way for the spirits, just like the wafting clouds of incense, to accompany them in their "ascent." The music of the meksa has a plaintive, insistent sound to it that some have likened to the blues.

The third and most important moment is the *derdeba*. It starts at midnight and goes on right through the night until dawn. This is the moment for the dances of the seven colors (one per spirit), led by the *moqadamat* and the clairvoyants. At the most intense moment of the lila, leaps and trances let the spirits into the magic circle, the wild *mlouk* who take possession of the gathering.

In the nearby Tafilalet, the Mahlun gives priority to singing and poetry. Accompanied by the *tbel*, the mountain drum, cymbals and the gembri or drum-lute, the cult instrument of Morocco, the minstrel-cum-storyteller improvises on sacred themes, or topics borrowed from the present day. The same goes for the travelling singers of the Atlas, as they interpret the *Rwayes*.

During the city-based moussem of Fez, on the pilgrimage to the tomb of Mawlay Idriss I and II, Andalusian and Granadan music strikes up in *nouba*, a succession of musical passages, which, ever since *Ziryab*, come in the same order—orchestral and vocal prelude, solo recital, song of love and frenzied finale.

Preceding pages: *Some groups of musicians pay tribute to their instruments by offering them dates. This shows the symbolic power of the genbri and other darbouka dispensing water, milk and blood, their decorated box a trap for spirits.*
Opposite: *In Morocco, music is not just made by men. They may hold sway in Andalusian music and the orchestral sections of the Sufi tradition, but as soon as you draw near the land of the Berbers, it is women who call the tune of the moussem.*

THE MEDINA

CITY OF ISLAM

The *medina*—al madinat in Arabic—is the preeminent city, the blessed city of Islam. To build it you need water, transported at great expense, as in Marrakech; timber, as in Fez; a rich nearby valley, unobstructed land, the *cheikha*, and a series of surrounding walls, whose crenellations and monumental gates are the most visible feature. Once within, the visitor enters into a succession of narrow lanes, corridors with sudden bottlenecks, covered passages sometimes leading to the great mosque—that essential symbol of the medina—beckoning from afar with its minaret. There can be no city without nooks and crannies, hideaways, dead-ends, porticos and soaring defensive walls. Whereas the layout of the surrounding wall and the erection of the mosque are the true foundation of the Islamic city, the medina cannot exist without its *souk*, the market, its enclosed *qissariya* and its *fondouk*, its storehouses and workshops. The medina only meets the requirements of the Koran if not far from the mosque the faithful Muslim can carry out his ritual ablutions in the *hammam* specially built to this end. The fountains supplying every neighborhood or *derb* with water must be equal to their task and be richly decorated with *zelliges*. The other principal features of the medina are the *medersa*, the Koranic schools where students or *tolba* live and study—these are particularly numerous in Fez and Marrakech. Nor could the medina fail to contain saintly sanctuaries and the headquarters of confraternities, the *zaouïa*—because every town and city in Morocco is beholden to one or more *marabouts*. Thus we find Mawlay Idriss in Fez, and the seven saints of Marrakech. Its size and importance are gauged against the *casbah*, the stronghold and the vast scale of the palace, often built on the edge of its ramparts, in order to extend its gardens so as to have enough room for the outbuildings of the *mechouar*. Nor would it ever infringe upon the rules of separation which require that residential neighborhoods be built away from markets and workshops, in enclosures which, at the turn of the 20th century, were still closed off by doors. From the 14th century on, the medina would accommodate Jews in the separate quarter known as the *mellah*. The medina must also be so designed as to preserve the privacy of each and every family, in the home's patio or courtyard, protected by the *horma* from the derb, the narrow street or dead-end alley outside, and by the unwritten laws of good neighborliness. It must ensure that the communal oven meets everybody's needs, as well as the little prayer rooms scattered throughout its streets full of shops. Its present-day revival, after many long years of neglect during which it came across as the very example of backwardness and unhealthiness, owes a great deal to its organic aspect—"...with the calm pace of footsteps" and "shoulder-height"—which so thrilled Le Corbusier.[1] You go to the medina for its secret pleasures, and the privacy of its riyad--the feeling of nestling in an architectural dream, before the modern age burst onto the scene, with all its acts of violence.

Opposite and following pages: *"Cretan labyrinth? elaborate structure made by Daedalus?" asks Juan Goytisolo in Makbara, "possible residence of a legendary Minotaur, brought back to life?" The medina is a world illuminated by a magic lantern, a thread running between several mazes.*

GLOSSARY

AÇALA: tradition, authenticity

ADOUL: notary

ADRAR: mountain

AGADIR: fortified granary

AGELLID: sultan

AGUEDAL (*agdal*): walled orchard garden

AHIDOUS: Middle Atlas dance

AHOUACH: Anti-Atlas and Souss dance

AÏD: festival

AÏD EL-KEBIR: sacrificial festival

AÏD ES-SEGHIR: festival marking the end of Ramadan

AILA: family (*kbira aila*: large family)

AÏSSAOUAS (*aïssaouïas*): religious confraternity in Meknes

AÏT: child, son of (*ibn, ben*), people belonging to the same community, tribe

AKH: milk

ALAWITE (*Alid*): descendants of Ali, Sherifian dynasty reigning from the 17th century

ALMOHAD: "unitarian", Berber dynasty that reigned from 1138 to 1258 over an empire stretching from Libya to Spain

AMIN: head of a guild

AMIR (*emir*): religious leader

AMIR AL-MOUMININE: commander of the faithful

ARSA: large enclosed and irrigated garden

ASALLU: thick soup

BAB: gate

BALEK!: be careful, watch out!

BALI: old

BARAKA: blessing, power of the saints and decendants of the Prophet

BAROUD: powder, passage of the horsemen in the fantasia

BASTILLA (*bestilla, pastilla*): puff pastry dusted with sugar and cinnamon, stuffed with young pigeon, raisins and almond paste

BAY'A: allegiance

BEHÎME (*hemar*): donkey

BENDIR: wooden tambourine with skin on just one side

BLED: conutryside

BLED EL-KHOUF: land of fear

BLED MAKHZEN: subjugated land

BLED SIBA: dissident country

BURNOUS (*selahm*): hooded woollen coat

CADI: lawyer, expert in Islamic law

CAFETAN (*caftan*): long tunic open at the front with embroidered buttons and braid

CALIFE (*khalifat*): lieutenant, deputy, successor

CANOUN (*kanoun*): earthenware stove

CASBAH (*kasbah*): fortress, fortified quarter

CHEIKAT: professional woman musician and dancer

CHEIKH: the elder, head of a village or confraternity

CHERIF (fem. *cherifa*; plu. *chorfa*): descendant of the Prophet

CHIRÂT: group of woman musicians

CHLEUH: Berber tribe of the Atlas

CHOUARI (sing. *chouar*): double bag made of palm fronds

CHOURA: consultation.

CIBAQ AL-KHAYL: game on horseback

CHOUF!: look!

DADA: grandmother

DAHIR: government decree

DAR: house, home

DAR AL-MAKHZEN: royal house

DERB: neighborhood lane

DERBOUKA: pottery tambourine

DHIKR: danced and chanted religious invocation

DHIMMA: protection of Christians and Jews

DHIMMI: those protected by the sultan (Christians and Jews)

DIR: strips of land between plain and mountain

DJAMI (*jami*): large mosque

DJEBEL (*jebel*): mountain

DJELLABA (*jellaba*): hooded cloak

DJIZIYA: special tax for Jews and Christians in Morocco

DOUAR: hamlet

EMIR: he who commands

FABOUR: tip

FANTASIA: warrior game on horseback

FARAJIYYA: large billowing shirt

FARNATCHI: hammam furnace

FARRAN : communal oven

FASSI: inhabitant of Fez

FATIT: bread made of semolina

FERM: fired and varnished ceramic square, cut in geometric form

FIQH: Muslim law

FIQIH: scholar, jurist, in Muslim law

FITNA: discord

FITR: breaking a fast

FONDOUK: hostelry and stables

FTOR: breakfast

GEMBRI (*genbri*): drum-lute, two- or three-stringed gnaoua mandolin

GHARB: western Morocco

GHASSOUL: Moroccan shampoo

GHAYTA (*ghîta*): wooden clarinet

GNAOUA: tribe hailing from Guinea, confraternity of musicians

GORFA: room built on a terrace

GUEDRA: terra cotta pitcher, musical instrument

HABBOU (*habous*): goods left in perpetuity (mortmain) to a confraternity

HAD (plu. *huddud*): frontier, limit

HADARIYYA: city-dweller, civilized

HADITH: sayings of the Prophet

HAÏK: large piece of cloth worn by men and women, measuring approx. 10 x 5 feet

HAMMAM: bath, streamroom

HANNA: henna

HAOUZ: plain of Marrakech

HARAM (*horma*): sacred, banned, illicit, mistake

HARIRA: thick soup

HARISA: hotpot

HARKA: rregiment on a campaign

HEM: depression

HENNAYAT: henna specialist

HIJAB: veil

HLAYKI (*hlayqi*): ring of spectators, something forming a circle

HOURIS: young girls

HUDUD (sing. *haddad* or *hdada,* derived from classical Arabic *had*): borders

IMAM: the person who leads the prayer, title given to the sovereign in his capacity as guide of the faithful

JAHILYA: pre-Islamic period

JEDID (*djedid*): new

JEEMA EL-FNA : gathering, square of the departed in Marrakech.

JINN (plu. *jnoun*): spirit, genie

JNAN (*jenan*): orchard, open garden

KHABBAZ: baker

KHAMSA: five, good luck amulet

KHEMIS: thursday

KHETTARA (*kettara*): underground channel, draining rain water

KILIM: carpet or rug woven by nomads in North Africa and Anatolia

KOUBBA (*kouba*): domed mausoleum

KOUYOU: gnaoua dance

KSAR (plu. *ksour*): fortified village

LA'B AL-BAROUD: game with powder

LALLA (*lla*): lady, mistress, form of polite address

LILA: overnight stay, gnaoua evening

MÂALEM (*bouallem*): master craftsman

MADFUNA: merchant's ornate slipper (babouche)

MAGHREB: west

MAHDI: spiritual leader or guide, preacher

MAHLUN: Berber song

MAKHZEN: concept of the distinct authority of the state government and the central power of dar-al-makhzen

MAKROUTE: semolina cake stuffed with date paste

MALIK (*malek*): king

MARABOUT: saint, holy man, or his tomb

MARRAKCHI: inhabitant of Marrakech

MASJID: mosque

MECHOUAR: palace outbuildings, large courtyard

MEDERSA: advanced Koranic school

MEDINA: Arab town or city

MEGOURASHIM: Jews deported from Spain

MEHALLA: long expeditionary column

MELLAH: Jewish quarter or neighborhood

MENZEH (*menzah*): pleasure pavilion

MERINID: dynasty hailing from the Zenata tribe of the Beni Merine, reigned over the empire from 1258 to 1465

MESARBLA: craftsman's babouche

MINBAR: preacher's pulpit

MIRHAB: niche in a mosque facing Mecca

MOGHREB: setting sun, sunset

MOKHAZNI: auxiliary agent of the Makhzen

MOQADEM: municipal official, steward

MOQADMA: sanctuary guardian

MOTASSEB: market administrator and judge

MOULOUD (aïd el mouloud): festival celebrating the birth of the Prophet

MOUNA: offering of food

MOUSSEM: traditional festival in honor of a patron saint or marabout (cf.) and trade fair, pretext for dancing, singing, games on horseback etc.

MSEMEN: cake filled with almond paste

MSID: local Koranic school, prayer room

NAÏB: sultan's representative

NOUALA: cabin, hut

NOUBA: musical passage, festival

OUED: river

QADRA: saucepan, pan

QA'IDA: etiquette, rule of conduct

QBAR: tomb, grave

QISSARIYA (*kissaria*): covered shopping center, fabric and clothing market

QRAQECH: metal rattle, gnaoua musical instrument

RABTI: inhabitant of Rabat

RAÏBI: yogurt

RAMADAN: ninth month of the Muslim year, fast

RAS EL MADAYBA: origin of solitude

RAZZIA (plu. *rezzou*): surprise attack

RIYAD (*riad*): house with inner garden or orchard

RWAYS: troop of singing musicians from the Souss and the Anti-Atlas, conductor

SAADIEN: Sherifian dynasty, hailing from the Draa valley, reigned from the mid-16th century until the arrival of the Alawites

SAGHRIR: decorated bread

SEGUIA: irrigation channel

SELHAM: burnous

SIBA: disorder, dissidence

SIDI: polite form of address for a man

SOUK: marketplace

SOUIRI: inhabitant of Essaouira

STAH: terrace

TAJINE: earthenware plate topped by a pointed, conical lid, dish that is braised

TAJINE SLAOUI: earthenware plate with lid, speciality of Sala

TALLUNT: Souss tambourine

TAOUA: hollow plate

TAQLID: conformist

TBEL: large drum

TBURIDA: powder

TEFOR: breakfast, low table

TOLBA (*tholba, taleb*): student in theology

TOSHABIM: native Jews from Morocco.

VIRDIE BARRANI: intermediate room in the hammam

WALI: governor

WEST ED-DAR: covered patio couvert, main piece of the house

ZAOUÏA: religious community, confraternity buildings

ZELLIGE (*zelliges, zillîg*): decorative facing with multicolored geometric forms, set in panels

ZERI'A: milk with melon seeds, hammam beverage

NOTES

THE GATE
1. Pierre Loti, "Au Maroc," *in Maroc, les villes impériales,* Paris, Omnibus, 1996, p. 15.
2. *Ibid,* p. 15.
3. *Ibid,* p. 50.
4. *Ibid,* p. 38.
5. *Ibid,* p. 39.
6. *Ibid,* p. 78.
7. *Ibid,* p. 68.
8. *Ibid,* p. 133.

THE IMPERIAL CITY
1. Leo Africanus, *Description de l'Afrique, tierce partie du monde,* Francfort, Islamic Geography, 1993, vol. I, p. 346.
2. Enrique Gomez Carillo, *Fès ou les nostalgies andalouses,* Paris, Fasquelle, 1927, p. 53.
3. Balthasar Porcel, *Méditerranée, tumultes de la houle,* Arles, Actes sud, 1998, p. 381.
4. Brice Mattieussent, "Marrakech graffiti," *in Marrakech derrière les portes,* Paris, Autrement, January 1985, p. 40.
5. Leo Africanus, *op. cit.,* vol II, p. 50.

TANGIER
1. "There are many ancient monuments such as capitals, vaults, crypts, a bath, an aqueduct, much marble and many dressed stones" notes Leo Africanus, *op. cit.,* vol. I, p. 243.
2. Jean-Louis Miège, *in Tanger, porte entre deux mondes,* Paris, ACR, 1992, p. 26.
3. Cf. *Les Clandestins,* Youssouf Amine Elalady, Paris, Au diable Vauvert, 2000. Rachid Tafersiti, *Tanger, réalités d'un mythe,* Casablanca, Zarouila, 1999. L. Akalay, *Les Nuits d'Azed,* Paris, Seuil, 1996.
4. Robert Briatte, *Tanger s'il y a lieu,* Paris, L'Entreligne, 1988, p. 132-133. "Tangier," writes Gérard Rondeau *in Tanger et autres Marocs,* "is to Bowles what Berlin is to Döblin and what Alexandria is to Forster and Durrell."

JEMAA EL-FNA
1. Juan Goytisolo, *Makbara,* Paris, Seuil, 1982, p. 174.
2. José Angel Valente, *La pierre et le center,* Paris, José Corti, 1991, p. 31.

THE SOUK
1. Jean-François Troin, *Les souks marocains, marchés ruraux et organisation de l'espace dans la moitié nord du Maroc,* Aix-en-Provence, Edisud, 1975, vol. I, p. 18.
2. *Ibid.*

THE MELLAH
1. *In* Haïm Zafrani, *Juifs d'Andalousie et du Maghreb,* Paris, Maisonneuve et Larose, 1996, p. 34.
2. Maimonides: codifier and theoretician of Judaic law, rationalist philosopher and physician; born in Cordoba in 1135, exiled to Fez in 1160, then to Cairo, where he wrote the Guide of the Lost.
3. Germain Moüette, *Relation de la captivité du Sr. Moüette dans les royaumes de Fez et de Maroc,* Paris, J. Cochart, 1683; forthcoming autumn 2001, Paris, Mercure de France, "Le petit mercure," presentation X. Girard.
4. François Pidou de Saint-Olon, *Estat présent de l'empire de Maroc,* Paris, Brunet, 1694 ; forthcoming too autumn 2001, Paris, "Le petit mercure," presentation X. Girard.
5. Pierre Loti, *op. cit.,* p. 118.
6. Jérôme et Jean Tharaud, "Fez ou les bourgeois de l'Islam," in *Maroc, les villes impériales, op. cit.,* p. 188.
7. Edmond Amran El-Maleh, in *Les Juifs du Maroc,* edited by André Goldenberg, Paris, Editions du Scribe, 1992, p. 199.

THE MOSQUE
1. Henri Terrasse, *Médersas du Maroc,* Paris, Morancé, 1928, p. 38.
2. Pierre Loti, *op. cit.,* p. 75.
3. J. et J. Tharaud, "Fez ou les bourgeois de l'Islam," in *Maroc, les villes impériales, op. cit.,* 1996, p. 243.
4. Philippe Ploquin and Françoise Peuriot, *La mosquée Hassan II,* Panayrac, Daniel Briand, 1993, p. 16.

THE KING
1. Mohamed Tozy, *Monarchie et islam politique au Maroc,* Paris, Presses de Sciences po, 1999, p 27.
2. Mohamed Tozy, *op. cit.,* p. 40.
3. *Ibid.*
4. Henri La Martinière, *Souvenirs du Maroc,* Paris, Plon, 1919 ; *in Archives du Maroc,* compiled and introduced by Jacques Borgé and Nicolas Viasnoff, Paris, M. Trinckvel, 1996, p. 188.
5. Walter Burton Harris, *Le Maroc au temps des sultans,* Paris, Balland, 1994, p. 135.
6. Pierre Loti, *op. cit.,* p. 79.
7. Mohamed Tozy, *op. cit.,* p. 298.

HASSANE TOWER
1. Abu Yusuf Yakub al-Mansur (1184-1199) defeated the Christians at Alarcos on 10 July 1195. But the Cross held on to Toledo and Cuenca. The "reconquest" of al-Mansur (the victorious) would be short-lived.
2. Berghouatta or Berrhouata, a Berber tribe of the Atlantic lowlands south of the Bou Regreg.
3. Leo Africanus, *op. cit.,* vol. II, p. 35.
4. Las Navas de Tolosa, defeat of the Moroccan troops of Mohamed An Nasir (1199-1213) by the coalition of the Christian monarchs Alphonse VIII of Castile, Peter II of Aragon, and Sancho VII of Navarre; this marked the start of the decline of the Almohad dynasty; in Bernard Lugan, *Histoire du Maroc,* Paris, Criterion, 2000, p. 99-103.
5. Charles-André Julien, *Le Maroc face aux impérialismes, 1415-1956,* Paris, Jeune Afrique, 1978, p. 485-486.

THE KOUBA
1. Émile Dermenghem, *Le Culte des saints de l'Islam maghrébin,* Paris, Gallimard, 1954, p. 97 ; and cf. *Vie des Saints musulmans,* Alger, Baconnier, 1943.
2. A gift, and sign of divine power imparted through the character, bearing, intelligence, courage, skill, moral vigor, and charisma of the person holding it. Hereditary among the descendants of the Prophet. Handed on by contact. Synonymous with good luck.

THE CAFÉ
1. Zette Guinaudeau-Franc, *Fès vu par sa cuisine,* Rabat, J.-E. Laurent, 1957, p. 78.
2. *Ibid.*
3. Omar Carlier, "Le café maure: sociabilité masculine et effervescence citoyenne," in *Cafés d'Orient revisités,* edited by H. Desmet-Grégoire and F. Georgeon, Paris, CNRS, 1997, p. 177.
4. Edmond Amran El-Maleh, *Le Café bleu, Zrirek,* Grenoble, La Pensée sauvage/Casablanca, Le Fennec, 1998.

THE HOUSE
1. Germain Moüette, *op. cit.*
2. Jean Gallotti, *Le jardin et la maison arabes du Maroc* (drawings by A. Laprade, photographs by L. Vogel), Paris, Lévy, 1926, vol. II, p. 56.
3. Kaddour Zouilai, *Des voiles et des serrures,* Paris, L'Harmattan, 1990, p. 68.
4. F. Légey, *Essai de folklore marocain,* Paris, Geuthner, 1926, p. 43.
5. M. Boughali, *La Représentation de l'espace chez le Marocain illettré, mythes et traditions orales,* Paris, Anthropos, 1975, p. 18.

THE PATIO
1. Jean Gallotti, *op. cit.,* vol. I, p. 87.
2. André Chevrillon, *Un Crépuscule d'Islam, Maroc,* Bibliothèque arabo-berbère, Paris, Hachette, 1906 (and Casablanca, Retnani Eddif, 1999).
3. Pierre Loti, *op. cit.,* p. 113.
4. Kaddour Zouilai, *op. cit.,* p. 82.
5. Fatima Mernissi, *Rêves de femmes, une enfance au harem,* Paris, Albin-Michel, 1996, p. 9.

THE TERRACE
1. Pierre Loti, *op. cit.,* p. 88.
2. Fatima Mernissi, *op. cit.,* p. 5-15.
3. *Ibid.,* p. 137.

THE RIYAD
1. Malek Chebel, *Traité du raffinement,* Paris, Payot, 1999, p. 166 ; *L'Imaginaire arabo-musulman,* Paris, PUF, 1993, p. 264.
2. Salah Stétié, *Firdaws: essai sur les jardins et les contre-jardins de l'Islam,* Paris, Le Calligraphe, 1984, p. 22. "The garden in the land of

Islam," writes S. Stétié, "runs from the outside to the inside, and from the inside even further inside [...] A symbolic place, needless to say, but the symbol, in the case in point, is only the go-between, in the end without reality, of a Real that is stronger than it, a real which alone is..."

THE DESERT

1. Louis Gardel, *Fort Saganne*, Paris, Seuil, 1980.
2. Roger Frison-Roche, *Djebel Amour*, Paris, Flammarion, 1978.
3. Jémia and J.M.G. Le Clézio, *Gens des nuages*, Paris, Stock, 1997, p. 74.
4. Odette du Puigaudeau, *La Route de l'ouest, Maroc-Mauritanie*, Paris, J. Susse, 1945, p. 37.

THE ATLAS

1. Jean Risser, *Atlas berbère*, Laboratoire d'anthropologie et de préhistoire des pays de la Méditerranée occidentale, Aix-en-Provence, Edisud, vol. VII, p. 19.
2. *Ibid.*

THE DONKEY

1. Pierre Loti, *op. cit.*, p. 55.
2. Adonis, *Le Temps des villes*, Paris, Mercure de France/Unesco, 1990, p. 67.

THE ARGAN TREE

1. Ernst Jünger, *Soixante-dix s'efface [1] 1965-1970*, Paris, Gallimard, 1984, p. 530.
2. Louis Emberger, *Les Arbres du Maroc et comment les reconnaître*, Paris, Larose, 1938, p. 271.
3. Mohammed Khaïr-Eddine, *Légende et vie d'Agoun'chich*, Paris, Seuil, 1984, p. 10.

THE PALM TREE

1. L. Gognalons, "Le palmier-dattier. Légende, histoire, croyances chez les musulmans de l'Afrique du Nord", *in Revue Africaine*, second quarter 1912, p. 203-217.
2. Alain Hervé, *Le Palmier*, Arles, Actes Sud, 1999, p. 23.
3. L. Gognalons, *ibid.*
4. *Ibid.*

WATER

1. Driss Chraïbi, *Naissance à l'aube*, Paris, Seuil, 1986, p. 14.
2. Claude Ollier, *Cahiers d'écolier, 1950-1960*, Paris, Flammarion, 1984, dated 25 June 1951.
3. Driss Chraïbi, *op. cit.*, p. 18.

MILK

1. Fatéma Hal, *Les saveurs et les gestes, cuisines et traditions du Maroc*, Paris, Stock, p. 157-158.
2. Charles de Foucauld, *Dictionnaire touareg-français, dialecte de l'Ahaggar*, Paris, Imprimerie nationale de France, 1951.
3. Fatima Mernissi, *op. cit.*, p. 216.

BREAD

1. In his diary kept during his journey in Morocco (18th century), Thomas Pellow observed that when Moroccans "...found a crumb of bread, they would pick it up and kiss it" before storing it away.
2. Fatéma Hal, *op. cit.*, p. 138.
3. Auguste Mouliéras, *Le Maroc inconnu*, Paris, Challamel, 1895-1899, vol. I, p. 80.
4. Fatéma Hal, *ibid.*

TEA

1. Prosper Ricard, "Sucreries de Rabat," *in Hespéris*, VII, 1927, p. 371.
2. G. Lemprière, *Voyage dans l'empire du Maroc et le royaume de Fez, fait pendant les années 1790-1791*, Paris, Tavernier, 1801.
3. Roland Barthes, *Incidents*, Paris, Seuil, 1987, p. 54.

TAJINE

1. Fatéma Hal, *op. cit.*, p. 77-78.

HENNA

1. Michèle Maurin Garcia, *Le Henné plante du Paradis*, A. Retnani, Casablanca, 1992.
2. Fatima Mernissi, *op. cit.*, p. 214.
3. J. and J. Tharaud, "Fez ou les bourgeois de l'Islam," *in Maroc, les villes impériales, op. cit.*, p. 226.
4. Michèle Maurin Garcin, *ibid.*

THE HAÏK

1. François Pidou de Saint-Olon, *op. cit.*
2. Gaëtan Gatian de Clérambault, psychiatre et photographe, edited by Serge Tisseron, Paris, Delagrange, "Les empêcheurs de penser en rond," 1990, p. 31-32.
3. J. and J. Tharaud, "Fez ou les bourgeois de l'Islam," *in Maroc, les villes impériales, op. cit.*, p. 185.
4. Prosper Ricard, *Corpus des tapis marocains*, Paris, Paul Geuthner, 1975, vol. VII.
5. Zyriab, Aboul Hassan, (Baghdad 789-Andalusia 857), a reformer of the life styles--art of entertaining, clothing, finery and make-up--and musical art at the court of Abderrahman II in Cordoba.

BABOUCHES

1. Louis Brunot, "La cordonnerie indigène à Rabat," *in Hespéris*, 3rd et 4th quarters 1946.
2. Théophile Gautier, *Constantinople*, Charpentier, Paris, 1853 ; *in Le Voyage en Orient, anthologie des voyageurs français dans le Levant au XIXe siècle*, writings compiled and introduced by Jean-Claude Berchet, Paris, Robert Laffont, "Bouquins," 1985, p. 527.
3. Leo Africanus, *op. cit.*, vol. II, p. 99.
4. Driss Chraïbi, *Le Passé simple*, Paris, Denoël, 1954 ; "Folio," 1999, p. 77.

THE FANTASIA

1. Eugène Delacroix, "Le galop volant" in the series of 18 watercolors offered to the Count of Mornay. Cf. *Fantasia*, 1832, Musée Fabre, Montpellier, and 1847, in the Frankfurt Kunsthaus.
2. Pierre Loti, *op. cit.*, p. 44-45.
3. Cf. Marie-Pascale Rauzier, *Moussems et fêtes traditionnelles au Maroc*, Paris, ACR, 1997, p. 58-64.

ZELLIGE

1. Oleg Grabar, *Penser l'art islamique. Une esthétique de l'ornement*, Albin Michel, Paris, 1996, p. 186.
2. Leo Africanus, *op. cit.*, vol. II, p. 109.
3. Oleg Grabar, *ibid.*

RUGS AND CARPETS

1. Prosper Ricard, *op. cit.*
2. Abdelkebir Khatibi, "Du signe à l'image", *in Le Tapis marocain*, with Ali Amahan, Casablanca, Lak International, 1995, p. 62.

HLAYKI

1. Elias Canetti, *Les Voix de Marrakech, journal d'un voyage*, Paris, Albin Michel, 1980, p. 117.

KHAMSA

1. J. Herber, "La main de Fathma," *in Hespéris*, VII, 1927, p. 209-210.
2. Edmond Doutté, *Magie et religion dans l'Afrique du Nord*, Paris, Maisonneuve et Geutner, new edition 1994, p. 325.

THE MOUSSEM

1. Marie-Pascale Rauzier, *Moussems et fêtes traditionnelles au Maroc, op. cit.*, p. 156-168.

THE MEDINA

1. Le Corbusier, *Journal général* (25.06.1931) quoted by Alex Gerber, "Le Corbusier et la leçon du M'Zab," *in* the conférence "La Méditerranée de Le Corbusier," Publications de l'Université de Provence, Aix-en-Provence, 1991, p. 56. Cf. Jacques Berque, "Fès ou le destin d'une médina", *in De l'Euphrate à l'Atlas*, Paris, Sindbad, 1978, vol. I.

BIBLIOGRAPHY

BASTIAN, Jean-Louis, *Chaque fête de sang*, Paris, Denoël, 1986.

BEAUCÉ, Thierry de, *La Chute de Tanger*, Paris, Gallimard, 1984.

BERQUE, Jacques, *Le Maghreb entre deux guerres*, Paris, Seuil, 1970.

——, *Nous partons pour le Maroc*, with Julien Couleau, Paris, PUF, 1977.

——, *Ulémas, fondateurs, insurgés du Maghreb*, Paris, Sindbad, 1982.

BERRADA, Mohamed, *Le Jeu de l'oubli*, Arles, Actes Sud, 1992.

——, *Lumière fuyante*, Arles, Sindbad, 1998.

BOUGHALI, Mohamed, *La représentation de l'espace chez les Marocains illettrés*, Paris, Anthropos, 1974.

BOWLES, Paul, *Un Thé au Sahara*, Paris, Gallimard, 1980.

——, *Réveillon à Tanger*, Paris, Quai Voltaire, 1987.

——, *Le Scorpion*, Paris, Rivages, 1987.

——, *Après toi le déluge*, Paris, Gallimard, 1988.

——, *Leurs mains sont bleues*, Paris, Quai Voltaire, 1989.

CÉLARIÉ, Henriette, *Un mois au Maroc*, Paris, Hachette, 1923.

CHAMPION, Pierre, *Rabat et Marrakech*, Paris, Laurens, 1926.

CHARLES-ROUX, Francois and CAILLE, Jacques, *Missions diplomatiques françaises à Fès*, Paris, Larose, 1955.

CHARMES, Gabriel, *Une Ambassade au Maroc*, Paris, Calman-Lévy, 1887.

CHEVRILLON, André, *Marrakech dans les palmes*, Paris, Calman-Lévy, 1919.

CHOUKRI, Mohamed, *Le Pain nu*, Paris, Maspero, 1981.

——, *Jean Genet et Tennessee Williams à Tanger*, Paris, Quai Voltaire, 1992.

——, *Le Temps des erreurs*, Paris, Seuil, 1994.

CHRAÏBI, Driss, *Le Passé simple*, Paris, Denoël, 1954.

——, *Une Enquête au pays*, Paris, Seuil, 1981.

——, *La Mère du printemps*, Paris, Seuil, 1982.

——, *La Civilisation ma mère*, Paris, Denoël, 1983.

DAOUD, Zakya, *Marocains des deux rives*, Paris, L'Atelier, 1997.

DELACROIX, Eugène, *Souvenirs d'un voyage dans le Maroc*, Paris, Gallimard, 1999.

DÜRRENMATT, Friedrich, *La Mission ou de l'Observateur qui observe ses observateurs*, Paris, L'Âge d'homme, 1988.

EL-MALEH, Edmond Amran, *Parcours immobile*, Paris, Maspero, 1980.

——, *Ailen ou la Nuit du récit*, Paris, Maspero, 1983.

——, *Jean Genet, le captif amoureux, et autres essais*, Grenoble, La Pensée Sauvage, 1988.

FOUCAULD, Charles de, *Reconnaissance au Maroc*, Paris, L'Harmattan, 1998 (1ᵉʳ ed. 1888).

GARDEL, Louis, *Dar Baroud*, Paris, Seuil, 1993.

GARDET, Louis, *La Cité musulmane*, Paris, Vrin, 1954.

GOYTISOLO, Juan, *Don Julian*, Paris, Gallimard, 1971.

——, *Chroniques sarrasines*, Paris, Fayard, 1985.

——, *Les Royaumes déchirés*, Paris, Fayard, 1988.

GYSIN, Brion, *Désert dévorant*, Paris, Flammarion, 1975.

HALDAS, Georges, *L'Intermède marocain*, Paris, L'Âge d'homme, 1989.

HARDY, Georges, *L'Âme marocaine d'après la littérature française*, Paris, Larose, 1926.

HERGÉ, *Le Crabe aux pinces d'or*, Paris, Casterman, 1938.

JULIEN, Charles-André, *Histoire de l'Afrique du Nord*, Paris, Payot, 1978.

——, *Le Maroc face aux impérialismes, 1415-1956*, Paris, Jeune Afrique, 1978.

KHAÏR-EDDINE, Mohammed, *Agadir*, Paris, Seuil, 1967.

——, *Le Déterreur*, Paris, Seuil, 1973.

——, *Une Odeur de Mantèque*, Paris, Seuil, 1976.

——, *Une vie, un rêve, un peuple, toujours errants*, Paris, Seuil, 1978.

——, *Légende et vie d'Agoun'chich*, Paris, Seuil, 1984.

LAÂBI, Abdellatif, *L'Œil et la Nuit*, Casablanca, Atlantes, 1969.

——, *Le Chemin des ordalies*, Paris, Denoël, 1982.

LAOUST, E., *Mots et choses berbères*, Paris, Challamel, 1920.

LAROUI, Abdallah, *L'histoire du Maghreb, un essai de synthèse*, Paris, Maspero, 1970.

LE CLÉZIO, Jean-Marie-Georges, *Désert*, Paris, Gallimard, 1980.

LEGEY, doctor, *Essai de folklore marocain*, Paris, Geuthner, 1926.

LE TOURNEAU, Roger, *La Vie quotidienne à Fès en 1900*, Hachette, 1965.

MAALOUF, Amin, *Léon l'Africain*, Paris, J.-C. Lattès, 1987.

MARCAIS, Georges, *L'Art musulman*, Paris, PUF, 1962.

MARMOL Y CARJAVAL, Luis del, *L'Afrique*, Paris, Billaine, 1667.

MARZOUKI, Moncef, *Arabes, si vous parliez*, Paris, Lieu commun, 1987.

MASSIGNON, Louis-Ferdinand-Jules, *Le Maroc dans les premières années du XVIᵉ siècle*, Alger, Jourdan, 1906.

MÉTALSI, Mohamed, *Les Villes impériales du Maroc* (photos C. Tréal and J.-M. Ruiz), Paris, Terrail, 1999.

MIÈGE, Jean-Louis, *Le Maroc et l'Europe, 1830-1894*, 4 vol., Paris, PUF, 1961-1963.

MONTEIL, Vincent, *Maroc*, Paris, Seuil, 1962.

MONTHERLANT, Henri de, *La Rose de sable*, Paris, Gallimard, 1968.

NASSERI, Karim, *Chronique d'un enfant du hammam*, Paris, Denoël, 1997.

——, *Noces et funérailles*, Paris, Denoël, 2001.

OLLIER, Claude, *La Mise en scène*, Paris, Minuit, 1958.

——, *Le Maintien de l'ordre*, Paris, Gallimard, 1961.

——, *Marrakch Medine*, Paris, Flammarion, 1979.

PACCARD, André, *Le Maroc et l'artisanat traditionnel islamique dans l'architecture*, Saint-Joriez, Atelier 74, 1979.

PERRAULT, Gilles, *Notre ami le roi*, Paris, Gallimard, 1990.

POTOCKI, Jan, *Voyage dans l'Empire du Maroc*, Paris, Maisonneuve & Larose, 1997.

RACHID, O., *Chocolat chaud*, Paris, Gallimard, 1998.

REVAULT, Jacques, GOLVIN, Lucien and AMAHAN, Ali, *Palais et demeures de Fès*, Paris, CNRS, 1992.

RIVET, Daniel, *Le Maroc, de Lyautey à Mohammed V*, Paris, L'Harmattan, 1996.

RONDEAU, Daniel, *Tanger et autres Marocs*, Paris, Nil, 1997.

——, *L'Appel du Maroc*, collective title edited by the Institut du monde arabe, Paris, 1999.

RONDEAU, Gérard, *Figures du Maroc*, Paris, Eddif, 1997.

SERHANE, Abdelhak, *Messaouda*, Paris, Seuil, 1983.

——, *Les Enfants des rues étroites*, Paris, Seuil, 1986.

——, *Le Soleil des obscurs*, Paris, Seuil, 1992.

——, *De quel amour blessé*, Paris, Julliard, 1998.

——, *Le Deuil des chiens*, Paris, Seuil, 1998.

SIJELMASSI, Mohamed, *Les Arts traditionnels du Maroc*, Paris, Flammarion, 1974.

——, *La Civilisation marocaine*, collective title edited, Arles, Actes Sud-Sindbad, 1996.

TAÏA, Abdellah, *Mon Maroc*, Paris, Séguier, 2000.

TERRASSE, Henri, *Villes impériales du Maroc*, Grenoble, B. Arthaud, 1937.

TINGAUD, Jean-Marc et BEN JELLOUN, Tahar, *Médinas*, Assouline, 1998.

VAN DER YEUGHT, Michel, *Le Maroc à nu*, Paris, L'Harmattan, 1991.

WHARTON, Edith, *Voyage au Maroc*, Paris, Gallimard, 1998.

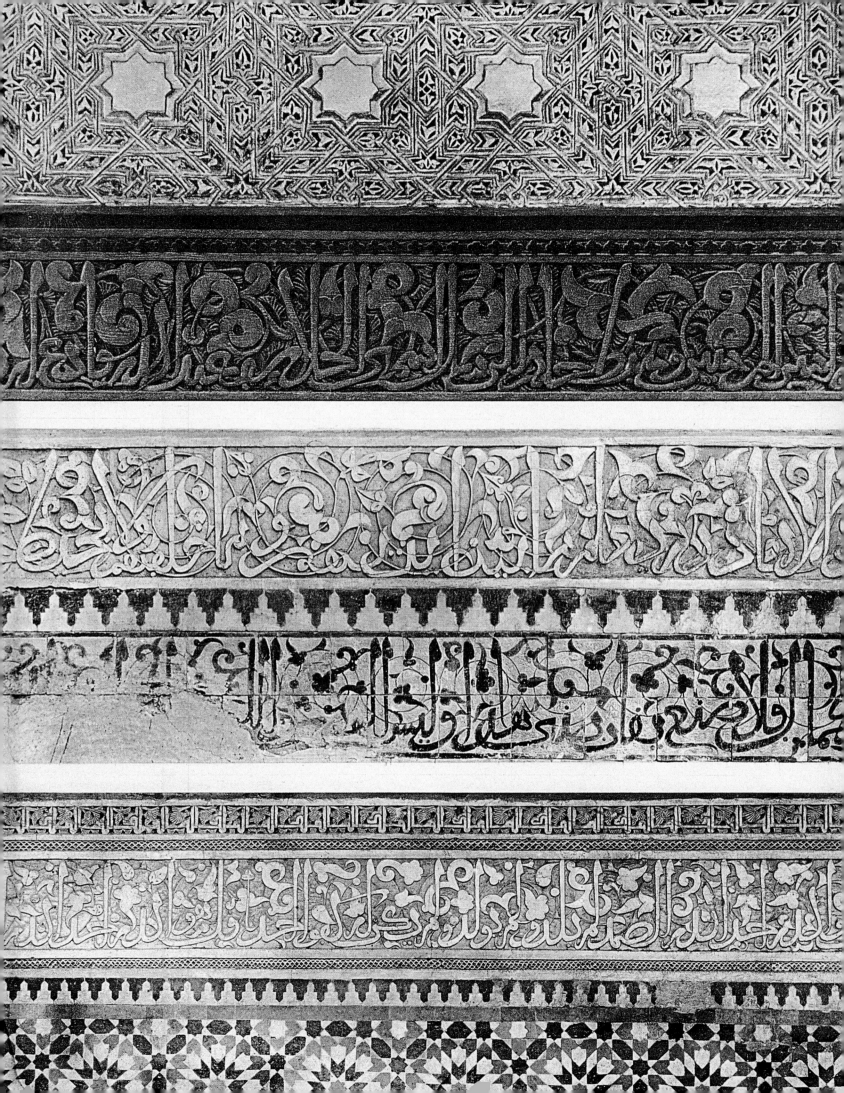

PHOTO CREDITS

p. 4	Harry Gruyaert/Magnum, Paris.	
p. 6-7	Collection Guy Joubert, Paris.	
p. 13	Bruno Barbey/Magnum, Paris.	
p. 15	Treal/Ruiz/Hoaqui.	
p. 17	Philippe Saharoff.	
p. 20-21	Collection Guy Joubert, Paris.	
p. 23	Philippe Saharoff.	
p. 25	Collection Guy Joubert, Paris.	
p. 27	Richer/Hoaqui, Paris.	
p. 29	Philippe Saharoff.	
p. 31	Collection Guy Joubert, Paris.	
p. 32-33	Dennis Stock/Magnum, Paris.	
p. 35	Harlingue-Viollet, Paris.	
p. 37	Musée d'Art et d'Histoire du judaisme, Paris.	
p. 39	R. Mattes/Explorer, Paris.	
p. 41	Bruno Barbey/Magnum, Paris.	
p. 43	Éditions Assouline, Paris.	
p. 45	Collection Guy Joubert, Paris.	
p. 47	Romain Contract/ Hémisphères, Paris.	
p. 49	Philippe Saharoff.	
p. 51	Romain Contract/ Hémisphères, Paris.	
p. 53	Bruno Barbey/Magnum, Paris.	
p. 55	Christian Heeb/Hémisphères, Paris.	

p. 57   Collection Guy Joubert, Paris.
p. 58-59   Bruno Barbey/Magnum, Paris.
p. 61   Collection Guy Joubert, Paris.
p. 63   Collection Guy Joubert, Paris.
p. 65   Stéphane Frances/Hémisphères, Paris
p. 67   Pascal Hinous/Top, Paris.
p. 69   Philippe Saharoff.
p. 71   Patrick Le Floc'h/Explorer, Paris.
p. 73   J. L. Bohin/Explorer, Paris.
p. 75   Philippe Saharoff.
p. 77   Collection Guy Joubert, Paris.
p. 79   Grégoire Gardette.
p. 81   Stéphane Frances/Hémisphères, Paris.
p. 83   Philippe Saharoff.
p. 85   Bravo/Hoaqui, Paris.
p. 86-87   Lafond/Rapho, Paris.
p. 89   Éditions Assouline, Paris.
p. 91   Bruno Barbey/Magnum, Paris.
p. 93   Laziz Hamani/Éditions Assouline, Paris.
p. 95   Collection Guy Joubert, Paris.
p. 97   Jean du Boisberranger/Hémisphères, Paris.
p. 99   Jean du Boisberranger/Hémisphères, Paris.

p. 101   W. Louvet.
p. 103   Collection Guy Joubert, Paris.
p. 105   Jean-Marc Tingaud.
p. 106   W. Louvet.
p. 107   Collection Guy Joubert, Paris.
p. 109   Bruno Barbey/Magnum, Paris.
p. 111   Collection Guy Joubert, Paris.
p. 112-113   Philippe Saharoff.
p. 115   Harry Gruyaert/Magnum, Paris.
p. 117   Philippe Saharoff.
p. 118   J. du Sordet/ANA, Paris.
p. 119   Collection Guy Joubert, Paris.
p. 121   Éditions Assouline, Paris.
p. 122-123   Collection Guy Joubert, Paris.
p. 125   Éditions Assouline, Paris.
p. 127   Philippe Saharoff.
p. 129   Bruno Barbey/Magnum, Paris.
p. 130   Philippe Saharoff.
p. 131   Jean du Boisberranger/Hémisphères, Paris.
p. 133   Collection Guy Joubert, Paris.
p. 135   Jean-Marc Tingaud.
p. 136-137   Bruno Barbey/Magnum, Paris.
p. 143   Collection Guy Joubert, Paris.

ACKNOWLEDGMENTS

The author is most grateful to Fatéma Hal, Abdellah Taïa, A. Jarif Saïd, Colette Fellous, Jean-Pierre Fouilloux, Chantal Thomas, Ali Madhavi, Jean-Yves Ravoux, Grégoire Gardette, the library staff of the Institut du Monde Arabe, Jean-François Mozziconacci, the Royal Air Maroc office in Casablanca, Martine Assouline, Véronique Billiotte, Véronique Botton, Julie David, the Bibliothèque publique d'information, the Bibliothèque nationale de France, Jean-Charles Blais, Michèle Cianéa, Hamed El Habib, as well as to Philippe Sébirot, Marie-Christine Biebuyck, Philippe Saharoff, Laziz Hamani and Jean-Marc Tingaud for their kind collaboration.